Raising a Talker

Simple Activities to Boost Language and Learning

RENATE ZANGL, PhD

RAISING A
Talker

Easy Activities for Birth to Age 3!

RENATE ZANGL, PhD

Gryphon House, Inc.
Lewisville, NC

Published by Gryphon House, Inc.
PO Box 10, Lewisville, NC 27023
800.638.0928; 877.638.7576 (fax)
Visit us on the web at www.gryphonhouse.com.

Cover photograph courtesy of Shutterstock Photography, www.shutterstock.com © 2013. Photographs by Annette Herz, Sriram Balasubramanian, and Shutterstock Photography, www.shutterstock.com © 2013.

Library of Congress Cataloging-in-Publication Data
The Cataloging-in-Publication Data is registered with the Library of Congress for ISBN: 978-0-87659-473-5.

Bulk Purchase
Gryphon House books are available for special premiums and sales promotions as well as for fund-raising use. Special editions or book excerpts also can be created to specifications. For details, contact the director of marketing at Gryphon House.

Disclaimer
Gryphon House, Inc., cannot be held responsible for damage, mishap, or injury incurred during the use of or because of activities in this book. Appropriate and reasonable caution and adult supervision of children involved in activities and corresponding to the age and capability of each child involved are recommended at all times. Do not leave children unattended at any time. Observe safety and caution at all times.

Table of Contents

Acknowledgments

My deepest thanks go to the many wonderful children and their families who have inspired and helped with this book.

To Laura Laxton and Stephanie Roselli, the editors of this book, thank you for all your insights and tremendous advice along the road.

To my husband, Sriram Balasubramanian, thank you for all your encouraging words and positive support in all that I do.

Introduction

Because many children seem to learn to talk and communicate without much effort, families and other caregivers often mistakenly think they can do little to foster this development. Not true! The more caregivers engage with infants and toddlers in meaningful, language-rich interactions, the more opportunities those babies have to build strong communication and language skills. Such early interactions pay off and give young children a head start. They result in better language skills and higher IQ scores at age three, and in more advanced cognitive and language skills well into the early school years. A child who can express herself well has an easier time making her wishes and needs heard, can regulate her emotions better, and can connect with people around her more easily. After all, we connect with each other most through language.

Raising a Talker examines how infants and toddlers learn to communicate, understand, and talk. Families and caregivers are so important in helping young children build strong communication and language skills. Everything a baby learns about her world she learns through communication with you, even early on. And science is clear: Enriched conversations with little ones matter.

The Science behind *Raising a Talker*

We know a great deal from science about how children learn to communicate and to make sense of sounds, words, and sentences. This book translates those scientific findings into concrete, practical tips that families and caregivers can use to jump-start communication and language learning and to better tune in to the needs and skills of young learners. These simple tips and strategies involve small, conscious efforts such as stretching words and exaggerating lip movements during face-to-face chats that make what a child hears and sees more memorable and easier to learn. But do not be fooled: *Simple* does not mean unimportant. These tweaks are communication and language catalysts.

A child's brain is malleable; it is shaped by her experiences. Learning experiences build upon each other. What and how much a child can learn from early conversations affect how she will learn from new experiences. Good communication with babies is central to their brain development.

The best time to start building solid language skills is in the first three years of life. Even as soon as a child's second year, big differences in language skills can emerge, as reported in a 2013 *New York Times* article titled "Language-Gap Study Bolsters Push for Pre-K." Researchers at Stanford University found that children from less advantaged environments lagged behind more advantaged peers at eighteen months, and by two years of age, these same children showed a gap of no less than six months. Researchers Hart and Risley estimate that children from homes where they are spoken to often hear **more than 20 million more words** by age three than children from homes where they are seldom spoken to. Since young children learn primarily from their families and caregivers, it is these early conversations, reading, and playtime that provide infants and toddlers with the perfect fertilizer for a great head start.

You can jump-start a child's communication skills by providing a language-rich learning environment from her earliest moments. You are much more than a bystander! You can shape and enhance what and how much she takes in, which affects how much she can learn—now and later on—and how she will communicate with you.

Providing a Head Start

Many families and caregivers want to give children a head start. They know that good verbal skills contribute to a happy and thriving child in preschool and beyond. Families often have questions as they seek to put their children on the right track:

○ When should I start talking with my child?

○ Should I talk in a singsong voice with my child?

○ Do I really need to repeat a lot?

○ When is the best time to start reading or to introduce the alphabet?

○ How do I introduce the alphabet?

There is a growing market of DVDs, flash cards, talking dolls, talking toys, and talking books. They sell well because they are marketed as having educational benefits for little users. But, are such gadgets the right way to help your child learn language and give him an early cognitive push? Research says no.

Researchers at the University of Washington took a closer look at videos marketed to babies, and their results, published in the journal *Pediatrics,* made headlines in 2007. Infants who watched so-called baby videos learned fewer words than their peers who spent the same amount of time interacting with real people. And fewer words is significant when you consider that these babies only have a handful of words in their vocabularies to begin with. It seems that younger babies are particularly vulnerable. In a 2010 study of children ages twelve to twenty-four months that was published in the *Archives of Pediatrics and Adolescent Medicine,* Richert and colleagues found that the earlier babies watch baby videos, the smaller their vocabularies.

What about other products, such as talking books? They may seem like a great idea; however, a closer look suggests that they cut into the quality of the conversations. Even though caregivers talk approximately the same amount of time as when they read traditional, nontalking books, when reading talking books they use many more directions centered on managing the child's behavior. They focus less on the book itself.

Talking toys are problematic as well. Even though a child hears lots of words as he hits buttons to make sounds and pictures happen, the words he hears most likely do not help his understanding. Why? Because he gets criss-crossed labeling—for example, when his toy spits out the word *duck,* he has already moved on to hitting the next button, which shows the picture of a cat. The timing is off. Babies who are starting to communicate need more than toys can offer. They need interaction with a person.

Language researchers Patricia Kuhl and colleagues designed a clever study in which they examined whether nine-month-old American infants learn Mandarin Chinese sounds better from real people or from recordings. In the study, Mandarin Chinese speakers read books with some infants live. Other infants heard and saw the same speakers read the same materials via TV screens. Another group of children just heard Mandarin Chinese speakers on audio recordings. It turned out that the infants only learned the sounds when they interacted with actual people. Audio recordings and TV sessions were useless for learning. Babies learn best when they see, hear, watch, and engage with real people.

It seems that young learners need face-to-face interactions to make learning experiences stick. A live person can immediately tune in to a child as he looks at you, points at something, or babbles. It is this well-timed back-and-forth between you and the child that gives real-life interactions that extra edge. Personal interaction shows a child that you are focused and with him, and that keeps him focused and ready to learn more.

The good news is that you already have everything you need: yourself—your vocal cords, eyes, hands, and fingers—and a desire to communicate with a little one. The baby is naturally interested in you and wants to understand and talk with you. She prefers your voice, your words, and your face over anything else from the time she is born. And she has enormous learning potential.

Although all learning rests on a complex interaction of genes and a child's environment, in language, the kinds of experiences a child has seem to have more impact than the genes. Researchers Robert Plomin and Philip Dale led an extensive twin study in 1998 with more than 3,000 two-year-olds. The study looked at environmental versus genetic influences in identical and fraternal twins. In typically developing children, the researchers found that the environment matters much more than the genes. The amount of interaction and the way caregivers interact with children is crucial. In another twin study, Stephen Petrill showed that the environment plays a key role in the development and growth of reading skills. This puts a lot of responsibility in the hands of your daily interactions and conversations with infants and toddlers. That means you can affect how a child learns to communicate.

Using This Book

Raising a Talker provides fun bonding activities and tools that encourage you to engage the child in your care in enriched conversations that provide the best possible foundation for strong language and communication skills. With little tweaks and conscious changes, you can easily and naturally transform play sessions into language-learning experiences and make your interactions more meaningful using practical, science-based tips and strategies.

> Babies learn language best from interactions with real, live *you*. Jump-start a child's language skills by engaging him in lots of face-to-face conversations: smile back at him when he smiles; wiggle the fluffy dog and say, "That is a dog," as he babbles; or engage in fun rhyming games. Your words, smiles, looks, and gestures are the strongest language-learning tools you have.

The sheer number of words you use in your daily interactions with a child helps build a bigger vocabulary. And quantity is not the only factor—quality matters, too. The way you speak with a child; how and when you say sounds and words; how often you tune in to and pick up on a child's babbles, words, and actions; and how often you ask questions all have a tremendous effect on how the child learns to communicate and to acquire language. It is that extra mile that gives those interactions the richness, support, and diversity infants and toddlers need to excel.

This book is written for use with typically developing children. However, the tips and strategies for supporting communication, language, and learning may be helpful for speech language therapists and caregivers who work with children who have minor language problems.

Raising a Talker provides more than fifty activities filled with practical, easy-to-use tips and strategies to build strong communication and language skills in children from birth to age three, the most exciting time in language learning. Each age range includes a brief overview of how children that age communicate and what aspects of conversation they pick up and work on. This book also discusses the cognitive, physical, and social-emotional changes that affect how a child communicates. Language checklists let you quickly track the child's growing communication and language skills at the end of each age range. Chapter 8 summarizes early warning signs of potential problems for each stage as well.

Early communication with a child is a delicate dance between the two of you, where one leads and the other follows, then vice versa. To better guide that dance and tune in to the child's emerging skills, *Raising a Talker* has easy-to-use goals, tips, and strategies for each activity. These encourage you to closely monitor conversation skills on both sides. This will help you become a more responsive partner on the fascinating journey into language. Keep the following in mind while playing:

○ **Have fun!** Building a relationship comes first. Infants and toddlers learn best when they have fun and enjoy their time with you. Learning follows naturally.

○ **Integrate language and play activities into your daily routines.** There is no fixed amount of time to play, but a child's brain thrives with repetition. That means that even if you are bored, a little one most likely is not. She is discovering something new that strengthens her understanding. Never push a child, use the tips and strategies as language drills, or exert any linguistic pressure.

The age spans in this book are general guidelines at best. There are wide individual differences between babies. The organization of the book offers loose recommendations on when to start certain language activities and what a child might tackle next, but it will not tell you exactly when he will reach certain milestones. Each child will learn to communicate at his own pace. It is your job to provide the best foundation for him. If you have concerns about a baby's language development, talk with a health professional.

○ **Be safe.** The activities are generally safe, but since young children explore objects with hands and mouths, put all objects and props away when you are finished playing.

○ **Provide downtime.** Babies need time to integrate and learn from their experiences. Watch the child carefully—she will let you know when she has had enough, even before she says words.

○ **Be flexible.** Adjust the activities to the developmental needs and stages of the individual child. The age ranges of developmental overviews and play activities refer to the *average* age when children go through the milestones and accomplishments. Each child will hit milestones in her own time. Many activities can be enjoyed much longer than during the age range given, often with minor adjustments.

After years as a language researcher, and having played with hundreds of infants and toddlers, I have learned one thing for certain: Infants and toddlers are smart communicators. They often make you laugh and ponder as their language lets you peek into their logic. I hope that the emerging language skills you witness will leave you with a sense of wonder and excitement about their thoughts, ideas, and feelings unfolding in front of your eyes through language.

The First Year:
From Gurgles and Sounds to Understanding

As you hold an infant in your arms and wonder what he understands, assume it is more than you think. Much language learning happens behind the scenes in the first year. It takes a baby a lot of hard, diligent work to reach the milestone of his first word. Thanks to research, we can say language learning actually starts in the womb.

A baby's brain nearly triples in weight in the first year, but what changes most dramatically is its wiring. A sophisticated network of neural connections is built in the first twelve months, and the construction of these connections depends greatly on a baby's experiences. As you connect with him in those first few months, you can affect his attention span, how easily and quickly he recognizes his name, and how he learns about the sounds of his language. Science tells us that how children experience language in the first year shapes future language skills.

The first year is an exciting one for the baby and for you. He learns that he can communicate with you, and you learn to understand him. He learns the basics of communication and figures out that his calls, cries, and experimental sounds have an effect: You respond and attend to him. And he thrives on that kind of responsive feedback.

He already takes in all kinds of information. He hears your words and observes your actions. He watches your face and listens to the tone of your voice. He cannot yet figure out what you say, but he soon knows what you mean by your tone and facial expressions. He even notices the sounds you make and how your lips change and move as you talk. He tracks the rhythm of your speech, such as how you pause at certain moments and speak loudly sometimes and more quietly at other times. He learns to carve up speech into structures, such as phrases and sentences.

In the second half of his first year, several big changes happen. He babbles more and focuses more on what you say and when you talk. He becomes aware that your words and gestures have meaning, and he starts to follow your eyes and your gestures more carefully. He plays with toys more and starts imitating you—not just your actions but also sounds and sound patterns. He begins to understand everyday situations and first words. Of course, his understanding is still on very wobbly legs, and he needs a lot of clues from you.

Interestingly, although he could pretty much differentiate any speech sound when he was born, he can no longer do so on his first birthday. His experiences from listening to you have changed his brain, which is now skilled in the speech sounds of the language(s) he hears regularly. In just one year, a baby has pulled himself from first gurgles to dissecting sounds to understanding first situations and words—an amazing feat!

From Birth and Up—Gurgles and Coos

1

Science Peek

Sarah came into this world just two days ago. She is lying comfortably and listening to speech, but not all of it is equally appealing. Sometimes she hears speech that is happy, with a high pitch that goes up and down. This is very pleasant and affectionate. Then she hears other speech, less happy and a bit boring, with a lower pitch and less variation in tone. She prefers listening to the happy speech, so she looks longer at the visual stimulus when she hears it. Regular adult speech is less exciting, so she looks away sooner.

Newborns love happy speech and singsong talk. Developmental researchers Robin Cooper and Richard Aslin showed that newborns engage longer when listening to baby talk. This suggests that it is important for families and early childhood specialists to use lots of happy, affectionate speech when talking with little ones.

Researchers have found that the way mothers sing with their babies is similar across cultures. They sing in an infant-directed style, using a higher pitch, a slower tempo, and clear emotions. Infants listen more attentively to this exaggerated style of singing than to other singing styles. They smile, vocalize, and stay engaged longer with adults who sing and interact enthusiastically.

Real-Life Story

Joe looks lovingly at his one-day-old baby, Henry, and wants to get Henry's attention. Joe slowly sticks out his tongue, making it longer and longer while moving it from left to right. He repeats the motion again and again, noticing that Henry's eyes are opening up more and his tiny tongue is coming out a bit, as if he is imitating Joe.

Andrew Meltzoff and Keith Moore discovered that newborns mimic behaviors they observe in adults' faces—from sticking out tongues to moving their heads clockwise to whatever simple actions they notice in the adult engaging with them. Learning to communicate through mimicking is one of a baby's strongest skills.

Newborns are incredibly smart and have tremendous capacities to track, compare, and mimic what they observe—all critical prerequisites for learning language. Babies are primed to communicate, and they do not lose any time getting started.

A Baby's Exposure to Language and the Environment

Babies first learn about language while in the womb. They remember something about the speech that they heard and will recognize it when hearing it for the first time after birth. This explains why a newborn prefers his mother's voice and her language over others. This seems to be true regardless of whether the mother spoke one language or two while pregnant. Babies also prefer listening to stories that were read to them before birth over new stories. Recognizing something in a world where literally everything is new is an important safety anchor.

Babies Love Voices, Faces, and Touch

We all communicate with more than our words. For babies, communication begins with loving smiles, gazes, and touches. Have you noticed that a baby enjoys staring at you, especially when you talk lovingly as you smile and gently stroke his soft cheeks? Your voice, eye contact, and touch are magnets for a baby.

Baby Talk

Many parents wonder if baby talk is good for babies. Science is clear: Baby talk is excellent language and brain food for little ones. When babies hear baby talk, they stay engaged in the conversation longer, are more attentive, and smile and vocalize more. Babies' brains are on high alert when listening to baby talk compared with adult talk.

Note that baby talk is *not* silly speech with made-up words; it consists of real words and real sentences spoken with a high pitch and singsong melody. When you speak in baby talk, you articulate sounds more clearly, drag out vowels, and pause longer between sentences. All of those traits make baby talk ideally suited to the auditory skills of infants who hear best the sounds that are higher in frequency, slower in tempo, clear, and distinct.

Coos and Turn Taking

Even though he cannot yet say words, an infant already has a pretty large wordless vocabulary that he uses to communicate. There are cries (increasingly differentiated to reflect different needs), burps, throaty grunts, gurgles, sighs, and first real sounds—called *coos*—which show up at about one month. A baby may coo a lot or rarely, for long periods or in short bursts. All of it is normal. Although his first vocalizations just happen, he soon realizes that they have significant power—they make family members and caregivers attend to him.

The best way to encourage a baby to communicate is to consistently and lovingly respond to his sounds, which sends the important message that he is noticed and heard. Good communication is all about turn taking. Your interactions with the baby teach him that people do not talk continuously, but they also pause, listen, and respond to others. Soon, you will notice that when you talk, the baby listens, and when you pause, he answers—flinging his arms, bursting into coos, and so forth. Your response likely will trigger another response from him, which triggers one from you, and the first back-and-forth exchanges emerge.

Does a baby already understand what I say?

Not quite yet; however, he does listen carefully to the tone of your voice, which carries your message.

When should I first start talking with a baby?

Right away. A baby's hearing is better developed than his sight. In fact, infants can discriminate any speech sound and are fascinated by human voices. He is ready to listen and learn.

Babies Begin to Smile

When a baby is just four to six weeks old, the first social smile may show up, triggered by chatting with or smiling at him. This kind of social smile is an important milestone. It differs from a spontaneous, random smile that he makes at the wall or the crib: It suggests that he sees you, realizes that you are smiling, and responds to it with his own smile. Social smiles make adults feel more connected and acknowledged, and they strengthen bonding.

Babies Become Interested in Objects

Sometime in the second month, a baby may start to swipe at objects close to him, using either his hands or his feet. Like his first sounds, his first swipes are accidental, but the effect gets his attention. This is the perfect time to hang brightly colored objects where he can reach them. He also starts to track objects with his eyes, although erratically. He will swipe at and track objects even more if you talk with him at the same time. You can use language to encourage his explorations.

Language Checklist 1: From Birth and Up

Does the child	Often	Sometimes	Never
attend to you and quiet down when you look at and lovingly talk to him?			
seek your face and the voice he hears by turning his head and moving his eyes and, later, his head?			
demonstrate a sucking/swallow reflex when using a pacifier or a nipple?			
respond to your voice with body movements, vocalizations, or smiles? make social smiles?			
vocalize with soft gurgling sounds or vowel-like sounds?			
seek other sound sources such as music, toys, rattles, and so on?			
respond in conversational pauses with gurgles, smiles, and so forth?			
mimic your facial expressions?			
make eye contact?			

Communication Tips

- ❍ Stay close (8–12 inches).
- ❍ Get the baby's attention through happy speech, eye contact, smiles, and gentle touches.
- ❍ Let him explore familiar voices and faces so he can learn to distinguish them.
- ❍ Mimic his vocalizations.
- ❍ Have face-to-face chats.
- ❍ Use baby talk frequently.
- ❍ Model turn taking, the back-and-forth of a conversation.
- ❍ Always pause to give him a chance to answer.
- ❍ Talk to him as if he can talk with you—treat him like a full conversational partner.
- ❍ Use body language (waving, kisses, and so on).
- ❍ Sing traditional and personalized songs.
- ❍ Let him listen to the sound of his own name.
- ❍ Deliberately set aside conversational times with him when you are not distracted.
- ❍ Play when he is alert.
- ❍ Give him downtime.

First Communication through Your Voice, Eyes, and Hands

Naturally curious, a baby wants to engage with you. You get his attention through your loving voice, tender gaze, and gentle touches. This starts a nurturing communication that makes him feel acknowledged, comfortable, and secure and fosters a healthy, strong attachment to you.

GOALS:

- ❍ Talk with the baby using baby talk.
- ❍ Give him opportunities to explore and distinguish familiar voices and faces.
- ❍ Provide one-on-one time with him.
- ❍ Make eye contact.
- ❍ Smile often.
- ❍ Give him opportunities for turn taking.
- ❍ Sing together.
- ❍ Let him hear his own name.

SKILLS FOSTERED:

- ❍ Body awareness
- ❍ Listening
- ❍ Social-emotional skills
- ❍ Visual skills

WHAT TO LOOK FOR:

- ❍ Does he respond to your voice through body movements, smiles, or vocalizations?
- ❍ Does he watch your eyes or mouth as you talk with him?

WHAT TO DO:

1. Sit with the baby securely placed on your thighs, his face oriented toward yours. Look at him and sing or say his name in a friendly, slightly higher tone than usual as you make eye contact: "Hello, **Harry.** How's my little **baaaby**?"

2. Your voice acts as a compass, orienting him to your face. Smile when he looks at you. As soon as he looks into your eyes, gaze lovingly back into his, and tell him how much you love him. Gently touch his cheeks, kiss his nose, and so on.

3. Rock or sway from side to side; this motion is soothing for him. Keep talking or singing. Your friendly voice holds his attention and relaxes him, and he learns about the sounds and rhythms of your language as you chat with him.

Infants are more interested in looking at a face that has looked at and talked with them. When you talk, your voice guides your baby to your face and holds his attention. In combination with your voice, your face makes the baby interested in you. He will gaze at you longer and likely vocalize more.

How Are We Different?

Listening and watching is where language learning begins and where a baby gets to know his caregivers better. For this activity, you will need two people. A deliberate switch from one person to another gives the baby lots to learn and provides some wonderful communication opportunities.

GOALS:

○ Give the baby opportunities to learn about voices and faces.
○ Let him listen to baby talk.
○ Help him recognize family members' and caregivers' voices.
○ Let him tune in to the rhythm and sounds of his language.
○ Encourage him to imitate and vocalize.
○ Help him explore and discriminate familiar faces.

SKILLS FOSTERED:

○ Auditory discrimination
○ Social-emotional skills
○ Visual discrimination

WHAT TO DO:

1. Have the baby lie in the crib or on the changing table, facing you.
2. Introduce yourself. Try to lock eyes while you speak using a friendly, affectionate tone: "Hi, Noah! It is me, your **mommy** (or teacher or aunt or brother). Your **mommy** is here! How do you like my voice?" Speak slowly and pause between sentences.
3. Talk about whatever comes to your mind: the weather, your favorite movie; it really does not matter. All that counts is that your voice sounds happy, that you articulate clearly and pause between sentences, and that you smile. After some time, say goodbye and move out of the baby's vision.
4. Let the other person appear and introduce himself. Move in to about ten inches from the baby's face, so he can see the person's face well. Start talking to get his attention: "Hi, Noah. It is me, your **daddy** (or teacher or grandfather or sister). What a surprise! **Daddy** is here, too! What do you think of me, my sweet little boy?"
5. Just keep talking, but pause deliberately at times so the baby can answer. He is not interested in nonstop chatter, not even as a newborn.
6. Switch back and forth as long as the baby enjoys the game. Because little ones like new experiences, the baby will give renewed attention to each change in voice and face.

WHAT TO LOOK FOR:

○ Does he become quiet and attend carefully to each person's face?
○ Does he respond to the voices and faces through body movements, smiles, or vocalizations?
○ Does he show renewed interest when he hears a new voice or sees a new face?

Newborns perk up and suck on a pacifier more when they hear their biological mother's voice. It is familiar, which feels good and safe in a world where there is so much new. It takes a couple of weeks for the baby to prefer Dad's voice over that of another male. This suggests that the speed with which babies recognize voices as familiar depends on the experiences they have had.

Let's Sing Together

Singing is probably one of the first and best language activities for a baby. What you sing does not matter; just sing often and do so in baby-talk style. Play around with volume and pitch, and see if the baby responds to these changes. Use his name in your songs, so he becomes familiar with it. Hearing songs and lines repeated helps him recognize the rhythm and, later on, chunks of phrases and words in songs he has heard over and over again.

SKILLS FOSTERED:

- Auditory discrimination
- Visual skills
- Body awareness
- Gross motor skills
- Social-emotional skills

GOALS:

- Get the child's attention through singing and saying the baby's name.
- Give him the opportunity to listen to the rhythm, sounds, and words of play songs and lullabies.
- Help him discriminate changes in loudness, pitch, and speed.
- Help him learn to recognize his own name.
- Let him explore faces during singing.

What Shall I Sing?

Adjust what and how you sing to the baby's state. If he is tired and about to fall asleep, sing a slow, soft lullaby with a low pitch and a soothing tone. If he is alert and energetic, sing a fast-paced song. If you feel shy about singing, hum a melody with a rising and falling intonation. By singing yourself, the baby gets a much richer sensory experience than recorded music can give him. He hears, sees, and feels you, which supports language learning and bonding.

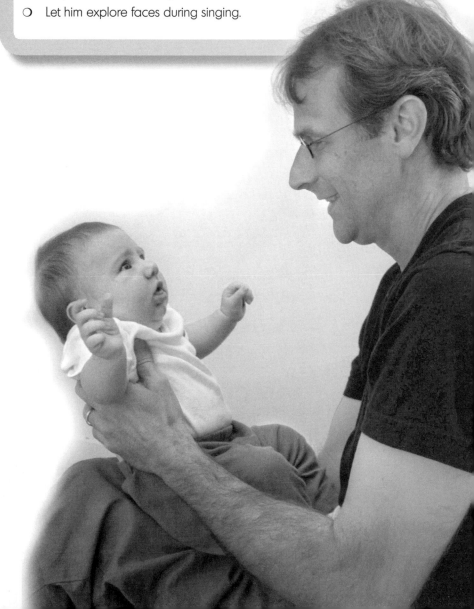

WHAT TO DO:

1. Sing popular lullabies as they are, or replace the names in them with the child's name—for example, convert "Mary Had a Little Lamb" into a touch-and-kiss song about body parts:

    > **Henry** *has a little nose, little nose, little nose!*
    > **Henry** *has a little nose that I am going to kiss! (kiss his nose)*
    > **Henry** *has a little hand, little hand, little hand!*
    > **Henry** *has a little hand that I am going to kiss! (kiss his hand)*
    > **Henry** *has little toes, little toes, little toes!*
    > **Henry** *has little toes, that I am going to kiss! (kiss his toes)*
    > *And everywhere that* **Henry** *goes,* **Henry** *goes,* **Henry** *goes,*
    > *Everywhere that* **Henry** *goes, Mommy is sure to go.*

    Continue with other body parts, touching and kissing them as you sing along.

2. Combine songs with gentle movements of body parts to promote body awareness and gross motor control.

    > *And* **Henry's** *left arm goes out,* (gently lift, stretch, and hold his arm)
    > *and* **Henry's** *right arm goes out,* (gently lift, stretch, and hold his arm)
    > *and* **Henry's** *left arm goes in,* (gently bring his arm back in)
    > *and* **Henry's** *right arm goes in.* (gently bring his other arm back in)

    Continue with his legs, moving them gently up, down, in circles, or sideways.

3. Create songs by simply singing about what you are doing. Integrate singing into your everyday routine.

4. Rhymes are ideal for language learning because of their words and simple melodies. Combine the songs with loving gestures to make them even more fun for the baby. Sing familiar rhymes, or make up your own.

    > *Tick* (touch the baby's nose)
    > *Tock* (touch your nose)
    > *Goes the clock and not the sock.*
    > *Tick* (touch his nose)
    > *Tock* (touch your nose)
    > *Another day goes by,*
    > *and I say hi!* (wave at him)

Nursery rhymes are a staple in young children's lives, but do they actually offer any benefits to children? Researchers Peter Bryant and colleagues found that, by age three, children who know more nursery rhymes develop a better knowledge of sounds and are better at spelling and reading later on. The repetition in a nursery rhyme heightens children's awareness of the sounds in words.

WHAT TO LOOK FOR:

❍ Does the baby respond to your songs through body movements, smiles, and vocalizations?

❍ Does he fall asleep when you sing soothingly?

❍ Does he react differently when you talk with him than when you sing?

My Turn, Your Turn

This activity promotes an essential of every conversation: taking turns. Since taking turns is so fundamental to any conversation, it is best to model and introduce the concept right away.

Exploring the merits of turn taking in early conversations, researchers found that turn taking primes babies to vocalize and communicate with caregivers. Three-month-olds who were engaged in typical turn taking vocalized more than their same-age peers who experienced random responses from adults. And, their vocalizations sounded more like speech sounds than noise. This means you can affect how much a baby vocalizes by carefully structuring your conversations to include nicely timed back-and-forth exchanges.

GOALS:
- Give the baby opportunities to learn the back-and-forth structure of conversations.
- Model appropriate turns and chiming in.
- Give him opportunities to vocalize.

SKILLS FOSTERED:
- Coordination
- Gross motor skills
- Listening skills
- Social-emotional skills
- Timing
- Visual skills

WHAT TO DO:

1. When the baby is alert, engage his attention. Comment on his sounds and reactions. Imitate whatever noise or expression he makes. At first, you may have to perform both roles: Ask a question, and then pause a few seconds before answering. A baby reacts more slowly than you do.

2. Wait for him to respond in some way. If he does not, answer for him after a pause of several seconds.

3. Extend and continue to comment on his sounds: "Is that what you think about last night? What an interesting idea you have!"

4. To encourage him to respond, raise your voice to a higher pitch, make a surprised face, smile, and look expectantly at him to clearly indicate it is his turn.

5. Accept anything as a turn—grunts, gurgles, coos, widened eyes, and so forth—and respond to it. Babies want to be noticed, and responding to their behavior encourages them to engage more.

6. Comment on his actions—for example, if he waves or wiggles his hand, pick up that hand and answer as you wave back at him: "Who is waving? It is **Alex**! **Alex** is waving." Again, notice if he answers your words and gestures.

7. Make a funny sound, such as clicking your tongue, clapping your hands, or snapping your fingers. Watch how he reacts.

8. Ask questions and touch the body parts you talk about—for example, ask, "Where is your **nose**?" going up in pitch on the last word. Pause for a few seconds, and then answer, "Oh, there is your **nose**," as you touch it. Or wiggle your fingers and say, "Here are my **fingers**. They're gonna get you!" as they approach and gently tickle him. Repeat the same sequence a few times, and then stop midway and wait expectantly with your hand still. See if he reacts.

9. Stick to the same structure and timing in songs, first games, and routines. Such repetition helps a baby understand the structure of conversations and anticipate when it is his turn.

10. Use popular nursery rhymes that incorporate actions—for example, play "This little piggy goes to market," as you gently tickle or massage each of the baby's toes. Pause after each toe and expectantly look at him. Create your own rhymes as well.

11. Play peekaboo. Look at the baby's face, and once he looks back at you, move your face back slowly while saying, "**Peeka**…" Move forward slowly, and when you are very close to him, gently say, "**boo**!" Stay within ten inches, so he can see you. Repeat the sequence a few times, and see how he reacts.

When can I expect a baby to take turns?

That depends on how often you model turn taking with and for the baby. If you do so from the beginning, he will have a good sense of it by about three months.

What counts as a turn?

Anything at this age counts—any sound, noise, action, or reaction by the baby, including crying, burping, staring, or widening his eyes.

WHAT TO LOOK FOR:

○ Does the baby begin to react in some way to your pauses, such as moving, staring, or widening his eyes?

○ Does the baby chime in with little noises? (The timing does not need to be perfectly coordinated.)

Three Months and Up—Vocalizing and Communicating More

Science Peek

Harry is comfortably hanging out on Mom's lap when a light blinks directly in front of him then stops. Next, he notices a light blinking on his left side, so he turns to look at it. Once he does that, he hears a friendly voice saying, "Peter, Peter, Peter," many times. After some time, Harry gets bored with this and looks away. Now the center light blinks again, so he checks it out. After it goes off, a light blinks on his right side. He quickly turns there and hears, "Harry, Harry, Harry"—his name! He loves hearing his name, so he keeps looking in that direction.

A team of language researchers wanted to know if four-month-olds can recognize their own names. The babies in the study looked longer at a light when they heard their own names than when they heard someone else's name. This finding shows the importance of addressing a baby with her name, so she can learn to recognize it. Babies recognize their names from about four months onward. Once a baby has learned the sound pattern of her name, she is able to memorize it, recognize it, and connect it with herself. Knowing one's name seems to be an important springboard to extracting other names from speech.

Mom holds out a toy cow and wants her little girl to reach for it. When Maya grabs the toy, her mom praises her exuberantly. Obviously thrilled about the cheery response, Maya smiles, kicks her legs, babbles, and waves the cow around. Then Mom changes the game a bit: She praises Maya in German and, later on, in French. Maya's reactions are the same. Maya goes by her mom's tone and face, and since they are so friendly, she reacts—regardless of which language she hears. At this age, babies start to understand you, but it is through tone and facial expressions, not actual words.

Experimenting with Sounds

A baby changes a lot in the three months following birth, and so do your conversations with her. This is due, in part, to her becoming more alert and active and making big gains physically, cognitively, and in her visual abilities. You can read each other's clues much better. Learning and imitating sounds is easier said than done and is a challenge for a baby because you cannot tell her what to do with her lips or jaw. She can only learn sounds by listening to you and watching your mouth.

Around the third month, the voice box, or *larynx*, which was originally high in the throat, starts descending. The baby has now more room in her mouth, can roll around her tongue more freely, and can create all sorts of sounds: vowels, raspberries, growls, gurgles, and laughs. Making sounds feels good, it gets your attention, and she loves to listen to her own voice. Babies this age also test how high, low, and loud their voices can go—sometimes letting out ear-piercing but happy screeches.

The baby is not just having fun with sounds but deliberately works on them, watching lips, listening to sounds, and imitating what she hears and sees. Observe how a baby scans your face; when you play face-to-face sound games, babies are mesmerized by the mouth. Your attentive, focused, face-to-face chats matter right now because she learns sounds and sound patterns through listening and watching your mouth and lips. She is driven to copy you, but it may be a while before she can do so really well. It is the effort not the result that counts.

Getting the Message

If you have regularly addressed a baby with her name since birth, she likely has heard it thousands of times. At around four to five months of age, babies start to recognize their own names. You will know that she recognizes her name when you call her from a short distance and she turns her head toward you or looks at you. She will not yet respond consistently, but she should be able to do so if you are close and there is no background noise.

Beyond recognizing her name, a baby at this age does not yet understand actual words. Nonetheless, she understands how you say things and what you mean by noticing the tone of your voice and your facial expressions. A baby begins to pick up on the emotions of others and starts to understand when someone is happy or sad. Your eyes, mouth, facial expressions, and tone of voice help her figure out how you feel, and she very likely will adjust her emotions. If you are cheerful, she will be more cheerful and chatty. If you are sad, she willl avert her gaze more often and engage less. Watch your emotions closely when you are with the baby, and try to stay positive. A baby needs clear, consistent, exaggerated signals.

If you have modeled appropriate turn taking, babies generally have a pretty good sense of the back-and-forth structure of a conversation by the time they are three months old. At this age, they will contribute to the exchange. A three-month-old soon will be able to anticipate her turn in songs that she knows well or in games that have a clear structure, such as peekaboo.

Babies continuously track cues in your speech, such as when you pause, when your voice goes up or down, what sounds and sound combinations you say loudly or quietly, what words you drag out at certain locations, and so forth. By four to six months of age, babies seem to have an idea of where one sentence ends and another begins, but they can only do so when they hear conversations in baby talk. Acoustic cues to those boundaries are more apparent in baby talk than in adult talk, which explains why baby talk helps them to carve up speech more easily.

Reaching and Exploring Objects

At three months old, babies love to get their hands and mouths on objects. A dramatic cognitive milestone—the ability to reach for things—makes that possible. Being able to reach for things gives a baby the chance to learn about objects: how they move, how they feel, what they taste like, and so forth. Use this newly found interest in toys to label objects for the baby as she explores them; this builds word memories over time. Playing games where she can grab dangling objects as you talk about them is the best way to foster language, thinking, and eye-hand coordination all at once. But, be cautious and watch out for potentially unsafe items.

Language Checklist 2: Three Months and Up

Does the child	Often	Sometimes	Never
like it when you talk, indicated by smiling, vocalizing, and so on?			
turn her head to locate the source of a sound, such as keys or a loud door?			
make and hold eye contact?			
produce sounds of pleasure and displeasure?			
actively search with her head or eyes to find the person who is talking?			
show social smiles and smile back when you smile?			
vocalize when you talk, moving her arms and legs as well?			
actively participate in a conversation, taking turns and talking back more with sounds?			
respond to her name by turning her head, smiling, or seeking you with her eyes?			
mimic your facial expressions?			
try to mimic your vowel sounds (the effort counts)?			
reach for objects, exploring them with her eyes, hands, and mouth?			
discriminate noises from one another, such as a plastic bag from keys?			
experiment with sounds in length, pitch, and volume?			
show different emotions?			
react differently to encouragement and prohibition?			

Communication Tips

○ Encourage turn taking through songs and games such as peekaboo that have clear signals for her to answer. Pause, look expectantly, smile, go up or down with your voice, and so forth.

○ Make eye contact when you talk.

○ Continue to use baby talk. Be animated and expressive in face and voice; talk clearly, slowly, and in short sentences.

○ Gradually increase the length of conversations.

○ Use your tone of voice and facial expressions to send clear messages.

○ Have focused, attentive, one-on-one chats where she can hear and see you talk.

○ Explore and talk about objects together. Talk about and name them as she plays with them.

○ Be attentive and tune in to her interests; pick up her gestures and vocalizations. Treat her like a full conversational partner.

○ Use body language such as waving, kissing, clapping, and pointing.

○ Sing often. Have certain songs for certain routines; accompany songs with actions such as clapping and waving.

○ Start reading board books or cloth books, ideally with bright, distinct illustrations and no text and one or two illustrations per page.

Seeing and Hearing Sounds

A baby needs to learn the sounds of her language. She needs to distinguish the sounds from each other, file them in categories, and figure out how to say them herself. By now she is well on the way to learning about sounds, playing around with her mouth and experimenting with delightful squeals. You help her learn about sounds by letting her hear sounds *and* see how they are formed.

GOALS:
- ○ Give the baby opportunities to listen to and watch the vowel sounds of her language.
- ○ Encourage her to imitate and vocalize speech sounds, so she can build up sound prototypes.
- ○ Help her discriminate sounds by hearing them and seeing how they are formed.

SKILLS FOSTERED:
- ○ Auditory discrimination
- ○ Cognitive skills
- ○ Fine motor skills
- ○ Visual discrimination

WHAT TO DO:

1. Place the baby in her infant seat or on the changing table, or sit her on your knees while you securely hold her. Make eye contact and get her attention by smiling, calling her name, or touching her gently.

2. Once you have her attention, start singing friendly /ō/ sounds, as in the word *no* and *snow*. Articulate the /ō/ sounds clearly by exaggerating your lip movements and dragging out the vowel. Repeat several times because, at this age, she needs time to process information. Have a break in between, and see if she mirrors you. She may need several seconds to answer.

3. Change the vowel sound. Sing friendly and animated /ē/ sounds, as in *see,* again repeating several times, exaggerating your lips, and dragging out the vowel. Does the baby imitate you during the breaks?

4. Switch back to /ō/ sounds, and after a while, back to /ē/ sounds.

5. After some time, give her something new to listen to, so she does not get bored. Combine the two sounds to an /ō-ē/ sound, and then alternate these with /ē-ō/ sounds. She may not imitate you right away, but she will do so over time.

6. Repeat each sound several times. A younger baby needs more time to process what she experiences than older babies do.

7. Mirror the baby as well. If she vocalizes, imitate her and then expand on it.

Is it important for the baby to hear and see me in this game?

Yes, absolutely. Stand in front of the mirror and clearly say an /ō/ and an /ē/ sound while watching your lips. You can hear the sound and see how it is formed. Hearing sounds and seeing how they are formed gives a baby two sensory draws, and this makes it easier to learn about sounds. Plus, babies who can see how sounds are made while they hear them imitate sounds more often.

WHAT TO LOOK FOR:

❍ Does she look at your mouth when you play sound games?

❍ Does she try to mirror what she sees and hears?

I Know My Name

This activity encourages a baby to listen carefully, recognize her own name, and locate sounds and voices at different distances. A baby's name becomes truly special for her when she starts to recognize it. Pay attention to how she responds when you call her by her name as opposed to an unfamiliar name.

SKILLS FOSTERED:
- Auditory discrimination
- Cognitive skills
- Locating sounds
- Memory
- Social-emotional skills

GOALS:
- Address the child by her name to foster name recognition.
- Encourage her to locate and orient to voices.
- Give her opportunities to visually track sounds.

WHAT TO DO:

1. Make up another name that sounds very different from the baby's—for example, if *Lena* is the child's name, use *Marvin* (both have two syllables but sound completely different).

2. When she is engaged in some activity, walk up quietly behind her so that she has to turn her head to orient to you. Call her excitedly by her name, and if she orients toward you, reward her with a kiss and play with her. Getting attention makes her realize that she did something special and motivates her to respond the next time as well.

3. At some point later, when she is engaged again, call her equally excitedly by the other name. How does she react this time?

4. Repeat this name game a few times. Does she respond differently to her name, which she has heard thousands of times before, than she does to the different name? If so, at what age does she do so? She may not respond consistently at first, but the more you use her name to call her, the quicker she will discover the special connection between her name and herself.

VARIATIONS:

❍ Different speakers: The baby's name sounds different when different adults say it. She has to learn to recognize her name no matter who says it. Play this game with different speakers to sharpen her listening skills.

❍ Locating voices: Place the baby in her car seat where she can still see you. Encourage her to track your voice as you walk to the left and right of her, calling her by her name. If she can follow you at this short distance, wait until she is engaged in something, and then quietly walk to a corner of the room and call her name again. Can she still locate you, despite the distance? Changing the distance pushes her thinking. She eventually will realize that voices sound louder when a person is close and quieter when a person is farther away.

> **Why is it important that a baby can recognize her name?**
>
> An infant listens longer to her own name than to an unfamiliar name. Hearing her name helps the baby to learn about it—once a baby has learned the sound pattern of her name, she is able to memorize it, recognize it, and connect it with herself. Knowing one's name seems to be an important springboard to extracting other names from speech. When she can recognize her name, the communication dynamic between you changes. She will more readily attend to you when you call her, and you can get and direct her attention more easily, which makes communicating with her easier. She will enjoy recognizing her name and the extra attention you give her when she responds to it.

WHAT TO LOOK FOR:

❍ Does she respond differently to her name than she does to an unfamiliar name?

❍ Does she stop what she is doing or orient to you?

Understanding Messages through Voices and Faces

This game promotes listening, learning about objects, and understanding messages through tone of voice and facial expressions. Learning to reach for objects is a major cognitive milestone. This is the perfect time to foster reaching and for getting "object talk" started. Tie your praise to the baby's action of grabbing the object, so she can learn the connection between the two. When she understands that she did something you really liked, she will want to do it again. Exaggerate your praise using baby talk, to make your message clear.

SKILLS FOSTERED:

- Auditory discrimination
- Cognitive skills
- Eye-hand coordination
- Listening skills
- Motor skills
- Social-emotional skills

GOALS:

- Give the baby opportunities to understand messages through tone of voice and facial expressions.
- Talk in baby talk and smile when you praise her.
- Help her differentiate among a variety of tones and facial expressions.

MATERIALS:

A bright object, such as a rattle
Ribbon, no longer than eight inches
Safety Note: Never leave a child unattended with the ribbon.
Preparation: Attach the object securely to the ribbon.

Use a prohibitive tone and a stern face when she touches something she is not supposed to. Her ability to understand that your tone of voice and facial expressions carry meaning will be important as she becomes interested in objects. It is best to reserve negative messages for safety reasons, so you can keep the overall communication positive.

WHAT TO DO:

1. Direct the baby's attention to the object. Move it, talk about it, and dangle it so it touches her hands and she can feel it. Say, "Look, there's a **bunny**! See the **bunny** hop? Hop, **bunny,** hop!"
2. Move the object away from her but still within her reach. Entice her to reach for the object by moving it gently.
3. If she grabs the object, praise her cheerfully with a big smile. You can praise her in another language or just nonsense words—it does not matter what you say as long as your upbeat tone and smiling face convey your message clearly.
4. Explore the object together. Repeat the game as long as she is interested.

WHAT TO LOOK FOR:

❍ Does the baby vocalize and/or smile when praised as she grabs objects?

❍ Does she react to prohibition by stopping what she is doing, looking away, not smiling, and so forth?

How does a baby best understand me?

Babies combine two sources of information when they try to understand you: your tone of voice and your facial expresssions. It is easier for the baby to make sense of what you say if your voice and your face send the same message. When the baby does something you like or approve of, praise her in a loving tone and with a happy face. When you want to stop her from doing something potentially unsafe, discourage her with a stern tone and face. Avoid inconsistencies, such as using a stern voice and smiling, that send a confusing message.

Six Months and Up—Babbling and Longer Conversations

3

Science Peek

Seven-and-a-half-month-old Andrew is comfortably lounging on Mom's lap. Then the show starts: Whenever a light blinks to his left or right, he looks in that direction. As he looks he hears a voice say the words cup *and* feet, *each several times. After that, instead of hearing just single words, Andrew hears full sentences, such as, "The cup was bright and shiny," "His bike had big, black wheels," "This girl has very big feet," or "The dog barked only at squirrels." Whenever Andrew hears a sentence with one of the familiar words,* cup *or* feet, *in it, he stays engaged longer.*

Language researchers Peter Jusczyk and Richard Aslin wanted to know if infants seven to eight months of age could recognize and remember words. They found that they can. Infants listened longer to sentences that contained familiar words, such as cup *and* feet, *than to sentences without those words. This means that at this age, infants reach an important language milestone: They have word memories and can pull out familiar words in conversations.*

Most likely, you have never been to Milpitas. I did not even know it existed until I visited some friends and their seven-month-old son, Mike. The dad was supposed to go to Milpitas, a small town about fifty miles southeast of San Francisco, and said something such as, "I have to go to Milpitas tomorrow." He noticed that Mike started to giggle and figured out that it was the sound of *Milpitas* that Mike found so funny. Every time his dad said, "Milpitas," Mike started to laugh so hard that his whole body shook, causing all of us to laugh with him.

Mike's laughs illustrate how children this age love sounds, have fun listening to words, and start recognizing words even when said by different people.

As you talk with a child, familiar words start to pop out to him, so label and talk about things as you play games, read, and sing. Repetition helps build word and sound memories. Recognizing a word is different from understanding a word. Recognition is the necessary precursor to understanding and is a very big language milestone because it allows a baby to build his vocabulary and learn about grammar. However, word recognition is far from stable at this age—background noise, a different voice, or a different tone can throw it off very quickly. At ten months old, word recognition will be much more solid.

Babies Change All Around

By now, a baby is reaching big milestones in language and in his motor, emotional, and cognitive development, which are all related to each other. Overall, communications are easier and more fun because you understand each other better. Although you can see some changes in his communication and language skills, a lot of very hard work goes on behind the scenes. The baby is furiously learning a lot about the sounds of his language, and his experiences of listening to you during the past six months are changing his brain. Let's look at the biggest changes.

Babies Start to Babble

Have you heard *ba, ma, da,* or even longer *dadadadas* coming out of the baby's mouth? If so, he has learned to babble and has reached an important language milestone. Babbling is putting a consonant and a vowel together in one syllable. Sometimes a baby will say short babbles, such as *ba;* other times he will utter whole babble sentences, such as *bababa* or *mamamama.* Babbling is his way of playing with sounds and language, talking with you, and directing and getting your attention.

Some babies may babble a lot; others less so. Some may start as early as six months; others not before eight. Regardless, this is a great time to start playing sound-babble games. Do not expect him to imitate you exactly—you will find yourself imitating him more often. Anything goes, as long as the back-and-forth continues. Just remember that some babies love imitating adults and some do not.

Da and *ma* are usually among the first babbles children all around the world say because these sounds are easy to produce and do not require much motor control. Although these early syllables do not mean anything or refer to anyone, they are more than random play. They are crucial practice sessions where he learns to control his lips, mouth, jaw, and breathing to get the sounds out. Of course, learning all the sounds is a big goal, and he is just beginning. Getting all the sounds right will take him about seven to eight years.

Even though these early babbles do not carry meaning, they are important. He needs the skill, coordination, breathing, motor control, and timing to string sounds together into "quasi-words."

Also, adults generally start talking back more once a baby says all these adorable *dadadas* and *mamamas*. Science tells us that your smile, affectionate pat on the back, responsive babble, or praise in real words can do wonders. These gestures seem to make babies babble more. The more often you respond to his babbles, the longer your conversations will be and the more he can learn.

Babies Make First Requests

Through vocalizing, reaching, or looking at things, a baby increasingly tells you in more sophisticated ways that he wants something. It is up to your observation skills to determine what that is exactly. Using speech sounds and gestures to make requests is a big step for a baby, because he realizes that they refer to something and engage your attention. Games in which you model how to request things encourage this skill. Understanding his requests will make your communication a lot easier.

Babies Tune in to the Sounds of the Primary Language

At this age, a baby makes gains in producing sounds and in perceiving them. Between six and twelve months of age, a child's ability to tune in to the speech sounds of his own language sharpens greatly, while he becomes less able to distinguish sounds outside of his own language. This is necessary for learning words because a baby needs to discriminate sounds that are important in his language. The better babies can discriminate speech sounds of their own language at this age, the better their language skills will flourish in the next few years. As you talk with a child, he learns about sounds and builds specialized brain structures.

Babies Untangle Speech More

When learning language, a baby has to break up the sea of sounds that he hears. At first he uses familiar names as springboards to finding new words and boundaries between words. He pulls out familiar words and recognizes new words that follow them. Around eight months of age, babies begin to use a more efficient strategy: They track conversations for *distributional regularities,* figuring out which syllables follow others and how often. For example, you probably have said statements such as these many times: "What a pretty baby you are," "There is my big baby," or "Where is my baby?" Hearing such sentences, a baby figures out that /bā/ is often followed by /bē/, so the chances are good that *baby* is a word but *bigba* and *myba* probably are not. Knowing which sounds are possible words helps him untangle the speech stream into words, which are easier to work with even if he does not know what the words mean.

Babies Begin to Understand Situations, Gestures, and Common Words

Does the baby get excited if you get the keys and move to the door? If so, it is because he anticipates going out. He understands the situation—even without words—just by your actions. He also may anticipate actions in daily routines that happen more or less the same way, in the same sequence, with pretty much the same phrases and actions. Generally, infants understand gestures and phrases before they understand single words. How do you know if a baby has begun to understand some gestures? If he waves as you say *bye-bye* or as you leave, or if he shakes his head to let you know that he does not want to give you back the remote control, that indicates understanding. Even though babies usually understand first common words at around ten months of age, some children are early comprehenders and understand some commonly used words before then.

Babies Learn Object Permanence

Understanding that objects and people are not gone when they are out of sight is called *object permanence* and is a major cognitive milestone. Peekaboo, hide-and seek, and dropping games where items or people disappear and then reappear will become his favorites at this age. These games allow him to incessantly verify his new understanding of permanence. Make these play favorites into language-rich games by linking actions and events with phrases, gestures, and labels.

Babies Copy Your Actions More Precisely

Babies typically love to explore objects and imitate what you do with them, and they do so specifically. If you shake something, he will shake it; if you roll something, he will roll it. If you exaggerate your actions, acting excited, then chances are that he will copy you. Play games where he can imitate you as you manipulate objects and talk about their noises and names.

A word of caution: A baby is not just a doer but also an increasingly quick mover. With his newly found ability to remember things, he likely will try getting to things that you have labeled no-nos, such as electrical outlets or your cell phone. Quickly redirect his attention from something he cannot have to something he loves and can play with. This keeps the tone of the conversation positive and his interest in communicating with you high.

Language Checklist 3: Six Months and Up

Does the child	Often	Sometimes	Never
babble, combining a consonant and a vowel, such as *ma, ba,* or *da*?			
have two or more vowels in his speech?			
have two or more consonants in his speech?			
experiment with sounds and babbles by changing his pitch and volume?			
search for a person he hears if she is not visible?			
protest when he does not want something, through gestures such as head shaking or pushing a toy away or through vocalizations?			
indicate that he understands his name, through looking at you or stopping what he is doing?			
understand the names of familiar people and actively look for them?			
actively participate in conversation through turn taking and speech sounds (not just through grunts or cooing)?			
play with and indicate interest in objects?			
imitate what you do with objects?			
respond when you babble or talk back?			
indicate that he understands gestures or situations, such as by waving when he hears *bye-bye*?			
indicate that he understands and anticipates familiar situations, such as by smiling before you appear during peekaboo or by chiming in when you stop a familiar song?			
look for items that are hidden?			
hold a conversation with you for a few turns?			
respond differently when someone is happy than he does when someone is sad?			

Communication Tips

○ Have lots of conversations—play games, read, sing songs, engage! Have one-on-one, face-to-face chats.

○ Avoid background noise from TV, radio, and so on when you are communicating with your little one.

○ Sing songs daily, especially songs that include simple actions that he can do, and match actions with words in the songs.

○ Read books to him daily. Point to the illustrations as you talk about them.

○ Listen, watch, and tune in: Respond promptly and consistently to speech sounds through affectionate gestures, smiles, babbles, or real words. Encourage speech by responding excitedly to his speech sounds rather than to all of his grunts and noises.

○ Follow his lead, his looks, and his gestures—and respond to him. Name what he is interested in.

○ Direct his attention by pointing at, talking excitedly about, looking at, or moving an object. Say, "Listen!" when you want him to listen or "Look!" when you want him to look at something interesting. This multisensory input helps him follow you.

○ Use baby talk: Be animated, stress important words, say shorter sentences, and repeat words and phrases.

○ Exaggerate actions and gestures.

○ Use familiar words and names often.

○ Label things and actions often to foster word memories.

○ Use self- and parallel talk: Narrate what you are doing and what the child is doing. The amount of speech children hear early on counts. Match actions and gestures with words: "Ah, you are rolling the ball"; "Let's wave" (as you are waving).

○ Get down on the child's level. Pick up a toy similar to his and play alongside him while noticing looks, gestures, and vocalizations.

○ Use your tone of voice and facial expressions to convey praise and prohibition. Send clear messages.

○ Deliberately pause in conversation and wait for the child to answer. Avoid talking constantly. Look expectantly at him and smile.

○ Treat him like a full conversational partner.

Recognizing New Words

Now that the baby has heard his own name or the names of certain adults thousands of times, he is likely to recognize them. Because babies use familiar words to carve up speech they hear and pull out new adjoining words, you can use the baby's name or your own as a springboard to draw attention to neighboring unfamiliar names—for example, those of toy animals or other toys the child plays with.

SKILLS FOSTERED:

❍ Auditory memory

❍ Eye-hand coordination

❍ Listening skills

MATERIALS:

Two of the baby's favorite
    toy animals

GOALS:

❍ Use familiar names of people to build baby's ability to recognize new words.

❍ Encourage baby to recognize familiar words and names.

❍ Carve up the speech stream by using familiar words as anchors.

❍ Connect words with gestures.

❍ Encourage imitation.

❍ Encourage vocalizing and turn taking.

WHAT TO DO:

1. Sit with the baby and hold up a toy animal. Say, "Look, there is **Trevor's bunny**" (use the child's name and the name of the animal). Emphasize the child's name and the adjoining word. Talk excitedly, in short and repetitive sentences.

2. Make the animal do simple actions that you talk about with the child: "**Trevor's bunny** is hopping." "**Trevor's bunny** feels soft." Continue to narrate the action and describe the toy, always using the child's name and the name of the animal.

   > **Trevor's bunny** *has very pretty* **eyes.** (Point to the bunny's eyes.) *See his* **eyes***? Where are* **Trevor's eyes***? What else does* **Trevor's bunny** *have?* **Trevor's bunny** *has furry* **feet.** *Do you want to feel them? Are they soft? Where are* **Trevor's feet***?* (Point at them.) **Trevor's bunny** *can* **kick.** *Look! He's* **kicking** *fast. Can* **Trevor kick***?* (Gently make the baby's legs kick.) **Trevor's bunny** *loves to* **wave.** *Can* **Trevor wave***?"* (Wave with the baby.)

3. Hold up the other toy animal. Say, "Here is **Mommy's doggie**" (use your name and the name of the animal). Make the animal do simple actions that you talk about.

   > *See what I have,* **Trevor***? This is* **Mommy's doggie***! Shall we play with him? Let's look at* **Mommy's doggie***. See,* **Mommy's doggie** *has legs and* **Mommy's doggie** *can dance.* (Wiggle the dog.) *Look!* **Mommy's doggie** *is dancing.* **Mommy's doggie** *can kick his legs.* (Make them kick.) *Now,* **Trevor** *kicks his legs.* (Gently make the baby's legs kick.) **Mommy's doggie** *can wave.* (Make the dog wave.) *Can* **Trevor** *wave, too?* (Help the child wave.) **Mommy's doggie** *can kiss.* **Mommy's doggie** *wants to kiss* **Trevor***.* (Kiss the child with the dog.)

VARIATION:

❍ Point out body parts as you use the child's name and the adult's name: "This is **Trevor's nose.** This is **Mommy's nose**," and so forth. Point at the body parts as you label them.

WHAT TO LOOK FOR:

❍ Does the baby vocalize and take turns at appropriate spots?

❍ Does he enjoy doing simple actions with you?

❍ Does he understand names of familiar people and first action words (*wave, bye-bye, clap,* and so on)?

My baby does not always respond to his name. Is that okay?

It takes a while for babies to consistently respond to even very familiar names. Seemingly little things, such as the radio or TV in the background or a slightly muffled voice, make it harder for an infant to recognize his name.

Babies learn to untangle your speech and find new words through familiar names, such as their own or the names they associate with familiar adults, such as *mommy* or *daddy*. Familiar names give the child an anchor among the sea of unfamiliar sounds and jump-start word learning.

Show and Sing

These activities encourage the child to listen, vocalize, and act out simple actions in songs with you, so he will learn to understand gestures and actions. A baby loves it when you sing with him, especially when there is action. By singing about what you do and repeating the same words and actions, you make him aware that your words and actions go together and mean something.

SKILLS FOSTERED:
- ❍ Balance
- ❍ Coordination
- ❍ Listening
- ❍ Motor skills
- ❍ Social-emotional skills

MATERIALS:
Scarf or ribbons (optional)
Safety Note: Never leave the baby unattended with a scarf or ribbon.

GOALS:
- ❍ Sing in baby talk to highlight attention to language.
- ❍ Talk about and act out simple gestures or actions.
- ❍ Encourage understanding of first gestures or actions.
- ❍ Encourage imitating actions and gestures.
- ❍ Encourage vocalizing and turn taking.
- ❍ Help baby become aware that sounds, words, and gestures have meaning.
- ❍ Match words with actions.

WHAT TO DO:
1. Make up your own lyrics, pick a well-known melody with a snappy rhythm, or invent your own tune. Many traditional songs—for example, "Pat-a-Cake," "The Wheels on the Bus," "Row, Row, Row Your Boat," or "Ring around the Rosy"—will work. Time your actions with the words, and as you repeat the song, keep the words and structure the same. Repeat the songs often, and show your movements clearly. Here's one to get you started:

Dance and Raise Our Hands
*Let's **dance**! Are you **ready**?*
*Let's **dance** and raise our **hands up**
high* (move the baby's hands up)
*Let's **dance** and raise our **hands up**
high* (raise his hands up)
*Let's **dance** and move our **hands down**
low* (move his hands down low)
Up high** and **down low! (move his hands up and down)
Up high** and **down low! (move his hands up and down)
*Let's **dance** and move our **hands out**
here* (move his hands to the left)

*Let's **dance** and move our **hands out there** (move his hands to the right)*

*Let's move our **hands out here** (move hands to the left)*

*Let's move our **hands out there!** (move hands to the right)*

2. Try this chant to help the baby connect gestures with words.

Wave Hello and Say Goodbye

*This is the way we **wave hello!** (*wave big with the baby's left hand)

***Wave hello!** (wave big with his right hand)*

***Charlie waves hello** here! (wave baby's hand to the left)*

***Charlie waves hello** there! (wave his hand to the right)*

***Charlie waves hello** everywhere! (wave both of his hands)*

You can also sing this song using the phrase **says goodbye.**

3. This is a fun chant to help the baby recognize his name and learn the name of a gesture.

Clap, Clap, Clap!

*This is how we **clap, clap, clap!** (clap with the baby's hands)*

***Mateo claps** here (clap to the left)*

***Mateo claps** there (clap to the right)*

***Mateo claps** everywhere! (clap while making a circle)*

*And a **clap** here (clap to the left)*

*And a **clap** there (clap to the right)*

***Mateo claps** everywhere! (clap while making a circle)*

4. Some other suggestions for simple actions:

   ❍ Bounce: Bounce him up and down on your knees, sometimes slower, sometimes faster. Say the word *bounce* as you bounce him.

   ❍ Pat: Have him touch a soft, fluffy toy animal. Use the word *pat* as the baby touches the animal.

   ❍ Kiss: Kiss the baby on various places. Say the word *kiss* each time you kiss him.

VARIATION:

After lots of repetition, freeze in the middle of your song and wait for the baby to chime in—for example, "Jacob **claps** here, Jacob (pause)." See what he does.

WHAT TO LOOK FOR:

❍ Does the baby participate with you as you sing songs with simple action words and actions or gestures?

❍ Does he indicate that he enjoys the activities, through smiling, vocalizing, or moving his body?

❍ Does he copy actions by himself (even rough copies are great)?

Infants listen more attentively to an infant-directed style of singing that uses a high pitch, a slow tempo, and clear emotions. They smile, vocalize, and stay engaged longer with adults who sing and engage enthusiastically.

Can I just do the actions without singing?

You can, but the baby will learn more if you sing *and* act. By singing, you add rhythm and highlight your words. It is the rhythm of your singing and your actions together that draw a baby into communicating with you longer. Singing may even help to build better sound memories.

Encouraging Babbling

At this age, the baby is starting to talk differently. His sounds are clearer, and he has begun to babble. What he needs is an attentive communication partner who babbles and talks back, encourages him when he vocalizes, and quickly and lovingly picks up vocalizations and responds to him.

Be especially enthusiastic in your responses to his babbles, not just to his grunts. He needs to learn that speech sounds are special. Start babbling away once you have his attention, ideally in one-on-one, face-to-face interactions. Articulate your sounds very clearly. Let him watch your mouth. The following are some sound games you can play to boost communication, sound learning, and listening.

SKILLS FOSTERED:
- ❍ Auditory discrimination
- ❍ Bonding
- ❍ Talking
- ❍ Visual discrimination

GOALS:
- ❍ Respond consistently and quickly to the baby's vocalizations and babbles.
- ❍ Help the baby to sharpen listening skills by repeating and varying sounds.
- ❍ Help him build sound categories.
- ❍ Encourage him to listen to variations in babbles—length, stress, and intonation.

WHAT TO DO:

1. Short and long babbles: Start out simple with friendly, one-syllable babbles that combine a consonant and a vowel (*ba, mee, po*). Do not be afraid to be a clown. Drag out the vowel and talk in baby talk. See if the baby notices your talk and responds. If so, immediately respond. If he gets into the game, say longer babbles, for example, repeat the same syllables a few times (*baabaabaa* or *meemeemee*).

2. Strong and weak babbles: Alternate *stressed syllables* (louder and longer) such as *BAAAA* and *unstressed syllables* (softer and shorter) such as *ba* to help the baby discern stress differences. You may end up saying things such as *BAAba BAAba baBAA!* This gibberish may not sound like much to you, but it is a great listening exercise for the child because real words vary in the way they are stressed. For example, when you say *BAA-ba*, the stress pattern is the same as in the word *DOG-gie*. Discerning and tracking strong and weak syllables is crucial for language learning.

3. Questions and answers: Say this out loud: *BA? Ba BA ba! Ba BA BA?* It sounds like a real conversation with questions and answers. Play around with raising your voice at the end of a word or sentence to make it sound like a question and with keeping it down to sound like answers. This lets the baby discern differences in intonation. Of course you can talk back in real words as well.

WHAT TO LOOK FOR:

❍ Does the baby vocalize when you talk with him?

❍ Does the baby babble?

His babbles do not mean anything, so why should I respond to them?

You should respond because your attentive and immediate feedback does wonders! It gets him to talk more and in a more complex way. You give a child's babbles meaning simply by responding to them.

Infants who can better discriminate the speech sounds in their own language at this age have better language skills in the second and third years and better prereading skills at the age of five. A child who can discriminate the speech sounds of his language may pick out actual words more easily and build his vocabulary more quickly than a child who cannot. All of this prepares him to manipulate sounds better when he gets ready for reading.

Since learning about sounds early on has long-term language benefits, engage in sound activities. Babies learn best when you both have fun!

Requesting and Labeling

These activities encourage a child to request things more efficiently, such as by vocalizing, looking at, and reaching for things. They also foster learning word forms, turn taking, and fine motor skills. Around the age of eight to ten months, babies have a new trick up their sleeves: They love dropping things and expect you to retrieve them. Rather than being frustrated by these often relentless dropping sprees, turn them into a wonderful language game by labeling the items over and over as you give them back to him.

SKILLS FOSTERED:
- ◯ Understanding of cause and effect
- ◯ Fine motor skills
- ◯ Gross motor skills
- ◯ Making requests
- ◯ Object permanence
- ◯ Spatial awareness
- ◯ Visual tracking

MATERIALS:

Some unbreakable toys

GOALS:
- ◯ Encourage him to request items through vocalizations, gazes, and reaching.
- ◯ Model requesting and reaching.
- ◯ Help him build word recognition through repetition.
- ◯ Label objects clearly and often.
- ◯ Give him practice at taking turns.
- ◯ Help him recognize names of often-used things.

WHAT TO DO:

1. Labeling: When the baby has dropped a toy such as a block on the floor, draw his attention to it and point to the object. See if he orients and looks at the toy or at you. Once he focuses on the toy, pick it up, wiggle it, and say, "Look, there's your **block**! Would you like to have the **block**?" Hold it in his general direction but wait for a response—a reach or vocalization—and then let him grab it. Use baby talk and name objects with their basic labels. Say, for example, "This is a ball," instead of "This is a soccer ball.

2. Requesting: Let the baby take the lead and direct your attention. How does he tell you that he dropped a toy and now wants it back? Any attempt other than crying counts: vocalization, reaching, or looking toward the toy or you. Waiting for the child to take the lead improves his communication skills by requiring him to make a request to get the toy back.

3. Build in surprises: Try to catch a dropped item in midair, and then hide it in your hand or behind your back. See if this surprises him; it is an unexpected outcome and challenges his thinking.

4. Reverse the game: Get his attention, and when he looks at you, push a toy such as a block off the chair. Now, model how to request a toy: Look back and forth between the toy and him, point at the object, and ask him for the block as you hold out your hand. He will learn that your back-and-forth looks between him and the object, your pointing at the object, and your asking mean, "Please give me the toy," even without understanding the words.

VARIATIONS:

❍ Put a toy on your head, label it as you point to it, and then nod your head so the toy falls off. Wait for the baby to grab, reach for, or otherwise indicate that he wants the toy. Continue the game as long as he is interested.

❍ After some time, check his ability to understand actual words by putting two familiar toys (for example, a duck and a ball) in front of him. Ask, "Where is the duck?" See if he chooses the toy you named.

Having a name attached to a novel toy focuses the child's attention on it and makes it more interesting. More attention may help the child to link words with objects. Have fun labeling things as you play.

I cannot figure out what the child wants!

It can be very hard to figure out exactly what a child this age wants. There are signs you can watch for that will improve communication: Look where his eyes are looking, see if he reaches his arm in the general direction of an object, and so on.

WHAT TO LOOK FOR:

❍ Does the baby follow objects with his eyes or by reaching when they drop to the floor?

❍ Does he look back and forth between you and the object that he has dropped?

❍ Does he vocalize to get your attention when he wants something?

Toy Talk and First Gestures

Babies are fascinated when things disappear and reappear. Match words with the accompanying gestures: Wave as you say hello or goodbye to a toy. Good timing helps him connect the gesture with the right word.

Why should I label things over and over? Isn't that a bit much?

What may seem like too much to you is not too much for a baby. Infants need lots of repetition to make word forms stick in their word memories. Researchers found that, after having heard words in recorded children's stories, infants memorized those words and were able to recognize them two weeks later. Since infants can recognize words from a recording, it is even more likely that a baby will remember words that you often say as you play and talk with him. The more you repeat and talk, the more chances he has to learn and memorize words.

GOALS:
- Help the baby attend to objects and the objects' names.
- Label object when you engage with the baby.
- Help him build word memories and word recognition.
- Help the baby understand gestures by linking them with words.
- Encourage the baby to vocalize.
- Encourage him to take turns.
- Encourage him to associate words with events, such as *bye-bye* with disappearing and *hi* or *hello* with reappearing.

SKILLS FOSTERED:
- Understanding cause and effect
- Fine motor skills
- Gross motor skills
- Object permanence
- Spatial awareness

MATERIALS:
Familiar toys
A big shoebox
Small piece of cloth
Scissors
Glue

Preparation: Cut an opening in the lid of the shoebox. Glue a little curtain over it using the small piece of cloth. Make the opening big enough so toys and hands can go in and out.

WHAT TO DO:

1. Draw the baby's attention to a familiar toy by moving it around and labeling it: "**Look,** Nathan, there's a **ball!**"

2. Announce what is going to happen next: "**Look,** the **ball** is going away! **Bye-bye, ball!**" Put the ball through the opening in the shoebox, and wave as you make it disappear. Once the ball is out of sight, say, "The **ball** is **all gone! No more ball.**"

3. Go through the same process with other toys, emphasizing the disappearance and the waving. Let him take over and put the toys through the opening himself.

4. Once all the toys are in the box, shake it with him. Look surprised by the noise, and say something such as, "**Listen,** Nathan! Do you hear something? There is something in the box. Let's see what is in the box."

5. Take out one toy, show it to him, wiggle it around, and excitedly label it. "**Look!** Here's the **ball. Hi, ball.**" (Wave to the ball.) The goal is to get the baby to take over and pull out objects. Help him if needed, and make a big deal when he takes a toy from the shoebox. When the baby babbles as he plays with the object, label it right then because his attention is clearly focused on it: "Yes! You're holding the **ball**, Nathan!" Repeat this game as long as he has fun, and introduce new toys over time.

WHAT TO LOOK FOR:

○ Does the baby vocalize or babble when playing with a toy?

○ Does he search for toys or items when they are out of sight?

Nine Months and Up— Understanding Words

4

Science Peek

Nine-month-old Katie is sitting on Mom's lap and watching pairs of pictures on a screen. Sometimes she sees a foot and some milk in a cup; other times she sees an apple and a mouth, then a nose and a cookie. As she looks, Katie's eyes are followed by an eye-tracking camera. Babies' eyes tell us what they already understand—for example, if Katie understands the word cookie, *her eyes—much like those of older children and adults—will look at the picture of the cookie.*

Babies understand many common names long before they can talk. Researchers Erika Bergelson and Daniel Swingley determined that children nine months old and younger already understand words for things they have had lots of experience with, such as food items and body parts when they hear a parent ask for them. This is the age where most babies' understanding gets off the ground.

Real-Life Story

When Sophia was about eleven months old, she heard her mother ask herself, "Where are my shoes?" Much to her mother's surprise, Sophia showed up moments later with one of her mother's black shoes in tow! Sophia clearly knew what her mother was talking about and thought to help her out. Sophia's mother asked aloud about her shoes a few more times during the next few days, and Sophia reliably arrived with her mother's black shoe and a big smile. Lots of shoe-related talk and play have taken place in that household because Sophia likes to hide things in shoes.

This story tells us a lot about children's word knowledge around this age. Babies know more than you may think and often will surprise you by suddenly holding out the item you were talking about. Their word knowledge is shaky and patchy, however, with more meanings to be filled in over time—for example, to Sophia, *shoe* may mean that black thing that goes on her mother's foot *and* a great place to hide things.

Communication near the End of the First Year

The biggest leap forward around this age is probably that the baby shows clear signs of understanding some words beyond the names of familiar people. Your communications are getting longer, and she has gotten very good at turn taking. She may even initiate conversations, show off what she can do with objects, start her own game of peekaboo or pat-a-cake, or arrive with objects in tow. She says a lot more, but much of it is still unrecognizable and seems to change quite a bit in meaning. Let's look at some of the biggest changes.

Babies Understand First Common Words and Phrases

Understanding common words is a big language milestone. The baby has figured out that grown-ups are not just talking for fun; their words mean something. They refer to people, toys she plays with, foods she eats, things she should not do, and so forth. Most babies understand their first words some time between eight and twelve months, and some even understand their first words between six and nine months of age.

The first words and phrases babies usually understand are names of people they love (*mom, dad*); words for moving things (*ball, car*); edible things (*juice, milk, cookie*); body parts (*nose, eyes*); animals (*dog, cat*); and words and phrases such as *all gone, more,* and *no*. In addition, a baby likely understands some sentences, such as, "Are you hungry?" "Give Grandma a hug," "Say goodbye," "Do not bite," and so forth. Every child's first vocabulary is different because children's life experiences differ.

Babies understand more than they can say. Saying a word is a lot harder than understanding it, because the baby needs precise control of her articulatory apparatus—her mouth, lips, jaw, and breathing—to get words out. A baby's speech is not yet articulated clearly, and one syllable often covers many different meanings.

A baby's understanding of a word differs from yours. To her, *dog* may only mean the dog she pets in her book and not the dogs that walks by her house, let alone all else that defines a dog for you. First-word understandings are often tied to one or two specific things the baby knows well. You can help her to generalize her understanding by labeling and comparing different objects with the same name, such as all kinds of shoes: the shoe in the book, the shoe on her foot, the shoe on the doll's foot, daddy's shoe, and so on.

> ## Making First Understanding Easier
>
> Follow the child's lead and label the things she is interested in, rather than redirecting her to what you are interested in or want to show her. Label the same things over and over again. Clearly and distinctly say the word in baby talk, in short sentences and phrases, or in single words. All these strategies focus a child's attention, draw it in, and highlight the connection between a word and its label.

Babies Understand More Gestures and Actions

Gestures that were rare earlier on, such as waving, now are in full swing—for example, only waving goodbye when somebody actually came or left becomes waving when she hears the word *goodbye*. New understanding of gestures and actions may even include talking on the phone, brushing hair, wiping, drinking from cups, and other actions babies have had a lot of experience with or have seen others perform.

Between nine and twelve months of age, babies are able to follow other people's gazes, pointing, and gestures. This crucial milestone in language learning allows a baby to determine where your focus is and what you are attending to. This enables her to learn about that thing you look at and talk about. It opens up a well of new information. The baby may also reach another milestone: *communicative looking*. She may shift her gaze between you and a thing she wants, and in doing so, tell you that she needs your help in getting that item. With this new skill, she can tell you what she wants, as long as you pick up on her looks and babbles.

Given babies' increased understanding of gestures at this age, some people wonder if this is a good time to encourage sign language. Signing is an efficient way for babies to tell grown-ups what they want, what they need, how they feel, and so on. Talking with hands and fingers is easier than talking with the mouth because it requires less muscle control and precision. The big advantage to signing is that you will be able to communicate sooner with a child, which can dampen her frustration at not being understood. Signing may also advance vocabulary and reading skills.

If you would like to start signing with the baby, this is indeed a good time to introduce sign language because she has the necessary fine motor and thinking skills to connect gestures with words. If you decide to sign, it is important that your signs do not replace your words because eventually she needs to learn words. Sign and talk at the same time, so she can learn what the associated words sound like.

Babies' Babbling Increases, Varies, and Begins to Take on Meaning

If you have noticed that the baby's talk sounds a bit like her native language, even though it is still mostly gibberish, you are probably right. She most likely is babbling in that language, because her "words" are uttered with its inflections and intonations. Babbling becomes language-specific around nine to ten months of age, just before babies say their first recognizable words.

At this stage, a baby's babbles vary more than before. She uses many different sounds that she strings together, saying exotic things such as *da-bi-koy* and *du-pu-doy* or still just plain old *dadada*. You can affect how much and how quickly her babbles advance by replying to those lovely speech sounds with words, babbles, and smiles.

Your feedback makes babies babble more and in a more complex way. Whether you respond verbally or nonverbally is not as important as responding quickly, consistently, and positively. In

2003, Goldstein and colleagues instructed mothers to affectionately respond within a second to their infant every time she made a speech sound, by moving closer, smiling, and touching her. After only ten minutes of this short but consistent intervention, the babies babbled more and in a more complex way. This led the reseachers to believe that quick and consistent social feedback boosts language learning.

Babies' babbles also begin to take on meaning now. **Treat babbles like real words.** Yes, it is hard to figure out what the baby means when she says *dada, DA*, and *dadada*. These little sound variations likely mean lots of different things. Even the very same "word" likely has many different meanings, especially when combined with the baby's evolving gestures.

So how do you interpret those early words? Consider this example: Maya said *da* while clenching a cracker and looking at it, and her mom said, "Oh, do you like that cracker?" Maya's mother did not look for the closest-sounding word in her child's vocabulary (*daddy*) but followed her child's focus—the cracker in her hand. The key to understanding those early labels and communications is to look for the child's focus and then interpret the word she said.

Babies Initiate Conversations

By combining babbles and gestures, a baby can now initiate a conversation. She may give you things or grab your hands or legs as she babbles to tell you that she wants you to read to her or give her the cup. She is likely to carry all kinds of objects to you so you will talk about or explore them with her. She also may start to sing as soon as you put her in the car seat or to initiate peekaboo or pat-a-cake.

Keep a diary of what words the child seems to understand. Watch how her understanding of words grows and what kinds of new words she adds. Also, videotape as you read a book together. Look and point at the pictures in the book. Can she follow you or even point to them herself?

Language Checklist 4: Nine Months and Up

Does the child	Often	Sometimes	Never
babble by combining syllables into longer strings—for example, *da dada* or *da ka di koypʊ*?			
vary babbles in pitch or volume?			
have two or more consonants and vowels in speech?			
protest through gestures and vocalizations when she does not want to do something?			
show interest in objects and have some understanding of what to do with them?			
show that she understands her own name, by looking at you or stopping what she is doing?			
understand the names of familiar people and actively look for them?			
understand specific questions, phrases, words other than *no,* names of people, and social routines—for example, "Where is Grandpa?" "Give a hug," or "Wave bye-bye."			
follow your hands and orient to objects that you point at and talk about?			
follow your gaze to look at the thing you are interested in?			
imitate what you do with objects as she watches you (rough copies count)?			
play or even initiate familiar games such as peekaboo, hide things and look for them, or engage in give-and-take games?			
understand what you want by your body language? For example, when you reach out with your open arms and say, "Come to me," does she move toward you?			
direct your attention to what she wants by vocalizing, looking at you or the thing she wants, or pulling you toward things?			
respond to *no* by withdrawing from what she is doing?			

Communication Tips

○ Investigate objects closely, demonstrating what do do with them.

○ Exaggerate your actions, and label and describe objects and actions as the child focuses on them.

○ Use language to give your play and daily routines structure and meaning from which the child can learn. Talk more now that the child is starting to communicate more. Good labeling and attentive, language-rich conversations are even more important than before.

○ Assume that the baby's babbling refers to the thing she is looking at, touching, or playing with. Label that object.

○ Respond to a baby's babble when she plays with a toy; the babble signals that she is really into that toy and very ready to learn.

○ Continue to reinforce turn taking and the back-and-forth of conversation.

○ For reading with the baby, choose books with bright, big, simple, realistic illustrations or photos and little or no text. Just one illustration per page is best. Books with baby faces, people, animals, and everyday objects are good choices. A baby "reads" through illustrations.

○ Use books that are safe and can be chewed on.

○ Books with flaps or other features that she can move with her fingers work well. Flaps are great because she can practice her new insight that things really do not vanish when out of sight. She can also practice her fine motor skills.

Reading Together

Reading is a great way to foster language learning and strengthen the bond between you and a child. It is a shared experience—it is all about being close, snuggling up, and having some great time together. Reading is *not* about reading straight through the book. In fact, starting at any page is good.

SKILLS FOSTERED:

- Understanding cause and effect
- Fine and gross motor skills
- Listening
- Object permanence
- Understanding

GOALS:

- Encourage the baby to follow your pointing and gaze.
- Encourage turn taking.
- Encourage vocalizing.
- Label pictures and encourage her to connect images with words.
- Help her with understanding first words.

MATERIALS:

Sturdy board books with bright and big illustrations

Pop-up books

Touch-and-feel books

Books that a child can manipulate

WHAT TO DO:

1. Establish daily reading times and routines. Read one-on-one, and eliminate background noise. Babies have a much harder time filtering out background noise than you do, since it directly competes with your voice and makes it harder for the baby to concentrate and hear you.
2. When the child indicates interest in a picture, label it for her.
3. Take your time and enjoy exploring and talking about the book together.
4. Read the same books over and over again. Repetition fosters learning, and children love familiar books.

WHAT TO LOOK FOR:

- Does the baby enjoy reading books with you?
- Does she vocalize or babble when she looks at pictures?
- Does she follow your gaze and point to pictures?
- Does she direct your attention to something she is interested in by vocalizing or shifting her gaze?
- Does she shift her gaze between you and the things in the book?

How to Share and Read a Book with an Infant

○ Be expressive with your voice and face. Exaggerate your tone of voice; speak higher.

○ Read slowly and enunciate very clearly. Smile.

○ Use simple sentences and single words: "Look at the **kitty**!" "Where is the **mouse**?" "See the **baby**?" Put the object name at the end of the sentence and stress it.

○ Add sound effects to the pictures: "That is a **cat.** It says **meow, meow**." "See, there is a **car—vroom, vroom**!" Children love silly sounds.

○ Talk in different voices for different characters. Hearing the cow talk in a different voice than the sheep or the dog will capture the child's attention.

○ Follow the child's interest—pay attention to where her eyes and fingers go. Point at and label the thing she is interested in (called *joint attention*). And watch your timing; word learning is about good timing at first. If you name the thing as she is interested in it, she can connect the picture and the word.

○ Listen to the child, and expand on her talk: "Oh, is that so? You are right! That's a baby!"

○ Repeat the same words and phrases often.

○ Connect pictures in the book with real objects. When you see a cup in the book, show the child her own cup and name it as well: "See, this is a **cup**, and this is a **cup**!" Help her learn that pictures and objects can stand for words.

○ Connect the illustrations to something personal—for example, the child's body parts: "See the **bunny**! Look, the bunny has **ears.** Where are your **ears**?" (Touch her ears.)

○ Let her turn the pages and shake and manipulate the book. Start reading wherever she wants to start. Reading upside down is okay, too.

When should I start reading to a baby?

The American Academy of Pediatrics recommends reading daily to a baby from six months onward. She is learning her first words, connecting words with pictures, and can focus on things at the same time with you. Even young infants engage with a book, making sounds and slapping or pointing at the pictures. Reading stimulates developing senses, memory, listening, and turn-taking skills. Children whose parents regularly read with them have language advantages over children whose parents do not often read. Reading helps build bigger vocabularies, the ability to think in more complex ways, and a better knowledge of sounds.

How about videos or books on tape?

Videos and books on tape cannot provide the one critical thing necessary for learning at this age: conversations with *you*, a live human being who connects affectionately with the avid little reader. She needs someone who smiles back at her when she smiles, talks back when she babbles, notices what she looks at and then talks about it—in short, someone who provides lots of loving attention and feedback.

Animal Talk: I'm a Tiger! Roar! Roar!

This activity encourages a baby to understand and imitate gestures and animal sounds. It also fosters babbling and word learning. Use animal hand puppets, giving them each a different voice and engaging in role plays with the child. Have the baby face you while sitting on your lap, or sit together on the floor facing each other.

SKILLS FOSTERED:

○ Gross and fine motor skills
○ Listening
○ Talking
○ Understanding

MATERIALS:

Animal hand puppets with movable mouths

GOALS:

○ Encourage her to babble.
○ Help her understand gestures, sounds, and words.
○ Encourage turn taking.
○ Connect gestures with actions.
○ Connect sounds and words with animals.
○ Encourage her to imitate actions, such as clapping, waving, and so on.

WHAT TO DO:

1. Introduce one puppet through gestures, animal sounds, and animal names—for example: "Hi, **Ariyana!**" (Wave, and then help the baby wave back.) "Who are you? Are you **Ariyana**? I am a **tiger.** Do you know what I say? Listen: I say **roar, roar**! Can you say **roar**?"

2. When she vocalizes, imitate what the child says, and then expand on it, using different sounds and words. Do not expect her to imitate you exactly—many children do not. They often imitate patterns they hear.

3. Entice her with some fun animal talk. Whisper sounds, and then say them louder. Drag out the vowels and make the animal sounds very distinct.

4. Stay focused on the child's face. Be creative, and whatever the child likes the most, keep doing it. Include simple actions that the baby can copy, and match them with corresponding words. This facilitates understanding.

5. Play peekaboo, letting the child find the animal when it is hiding behind your back.

6. Introduce other animal puppets one at a time. Follow the same overall structure as before, combining simple gestures, animal sounds, and their names—for example, "I'm the **cow**! I say **moooo, mooooo**!" or "I'm the **duck**! I say **quack, quack**!" Exaggerate both the words and the actions.

Quick and consistent social feedback boosts language learning. Babies babble more and in a more complex way when you respond quickly and affectionately, smiling, saying a loving word or babble, or patting the child on the back—it does not matter as long as you are consistent and responsive.

Can I just call the cow a moo moo?

You can, but it is best to use the word *cow* for the animal and *moo moo* for the sound it makes. This way, the baby can learn both. Babies often say the animals' sounds before they say the animals' names because making the sounds often requires less motor control.

Tuning In

This game promotes learning names for objects and encourages you to follow a child's attention. Joint attention fosters word learning by sharing the focus with a child and then labeling the thing that she is interested in. When learning first words, children learn more quickly when adults label objects correctly and at the right time.

SKILLS FOSTERED:

❍ Cognitive skills
❍ Listening
❍ Motor skills
❍ Understanding

MATERIALS:

Any toy the child is interested in (for tossing, use a toy that she can grab easily)

WHAT TO LOOK FOR:

❍ Does the baby try to get your attention when she wants something, by looking, pointing, or vocalizing?
❍ Does she stay interested in a toy when you label and explore it with her?

GOALS:

❍ Help her understand first common words using joint attention.
❍ Connect a familiar sound with a familiar object.
❍ Encourage her to attend and integrate cues: gazing and pointing, object and name of object.
❍ Help her understand that things have names.

WHAT TO DO:

1. At first, it is best if you follow the child's lead and pick up her interest—for example, if you hold a frog and she looks at it, you then look at the child, look at the frog, point at it, and then label it.
2. Talk about the frog as the child looks at it. "This is **frog**. It says **ribbit, ribbit**!"
3. Wait for her response, expand on it, and then label the frog again while describing it. Make the label "pop" by stressing the speech, making it longer, and putting it at the end of the sentence.

Do I really need to look at the thing when I talk about it?

Looking at a thing while talking about it facilitates word learning when a child is just starting to understand first words. It shows the child that your focus is on the same thing as hers. Dare Baldwin's 1991 study explored whether parents or caregivers are attentive to what a baby is focusing on and label what the baby is attending to. She found that they are quite good at establishing joint attention and that they label an object their babies are already focused on about 50–70 percent of the time. This follow-in labeling—as opposed to directing the child's attention to an object and then labeling it—seems to pay off.

Follow My Eyes and Fingers

This activity encourages the child to follow your focus to an interesting object that pops up and will be named, which fosters word learning. Her eyes start to follow your eyes and pointing to join your line of attention, skills that are very helpful in daily communications.

GOALS:

❍ Use looks and pointing to highlight objects and build an understanding of object names.

❍ Encourage the baby to follow people's gazes and gestures.

❍ Encourage the baby to tune in to someone else's focus.

❍ Encourage her to vocalize.

❍ Help her recognize and understand common names of familiar toys.

SKILLS FOSTERED:

❍ Fine and gross motor skills

❍ Listening

❍ Object permanence

❍ Understanding

MATERIALS:

2 plastic buckets

2 different toys

Preparation: Put a toy in each of the buckets. Put one bucket to the right of you and the other one to your left. Have the baby sit across from you.

WHAT TO DO:

1. Say, "**Look, Sara**," and then look and point at the bucket to your left. Turn your head very clearly toward it. See if she follows you.

2. If so, take out the toy and talk about it. Label it excitedly, and give it to her as she moves toward the bucket. Play with the toy together. If she is not following you, start over. This time, tap on the bucket to direct her attention to it as you point and look at it.

3. Say again, "**Look Sara**," but this time look at *and* point to the bucket to your right, turning your head very clearly toward that bucket. Repeat the same steps as described before.

4. Repeat this activity with different toys, randomly switching sides, so she gets used to following your gaze. Use a familiar toy with a new twist— for example, a block with a happy face drawn on it, or use a new ball the baby has not seen before. She will learn that it is worth following your look because there is something interesting to see and play with.

WHAT TO LOOK FOR:

❍ Does she follow your gazes and gestures to things that are close by?

❍ Does she follow your gazes and gestures to more distant things, such as objects outside the window?

❍ Does she vocalize and use gestures to direct your attention to something interesting she wants to share?

Follow My Eyes and Fingers (continued)

Why is it important that a baby follows my gaze?
When we shift our gaze and gesture toward something, we usually do so because we find something interesting and then talk about it. If the baby can follow you, she can learn about the thing you find so interesting. Early nonverbal communication skills, such as following another's gaze and pointing, are important for later language development.

Treasure Hunt

This game promotes babbling; word learning; and understanding of words, questions, and gestures. A baby this age loves peekaboo-style games, so hide objects under buckets and label them as you discover them together. Include empty buckets, so it becomes a real treasure hunt and allows you to talk about nonexistent things as well. Start simple, and add toys and buckets as you play.

GOALS:

- Help the baby understand first common words and gestures.
- Help her understand question frames—for example, "Where is the___?" means "Look for something."
- Help her learn about *all gone* and *no,* referring to nonexistent things: "The car is **all gone. No more** car."
- Encourage the baby to babble.

SKILLS FOSTERED:

- Understanding cause and effect
- Fine motor skills
- Listening
- Understanding
- Talking

MATERIALS:

2–4 buckets

Familiar toys

WHAT TO DO:

1. One toy and one bucket: Label a toy and hide it under a bucket as the child watches you. Say, "**Look**! There's your **car**! **Look** where the **car** goes! **Goodbye, car!**" Wave goodbye to the car. Put it under the bucket and say, "Uh oh! The **car** is **all gone**!" Look surprised, opening your hands wide. Ask, "Where is the **car**?" If she uncovers the toy herself, praise her excitedly, smile, and label the object right then: "**Look**, the **car**!" If she does not search for the car herself, help her find it. Repeat this activity as long as she is having fun.

2. Three toys of the same kind and three buckets: First hide toys, such as fish, under every bucket. Start the game and ask, "Where is a **fish**? Can you find the **fish**?" When she uncovers the fish, label the toy excitedly with a big smile on your face. "Oh, **look**—a **fish**!" When she finds another one, say, "Oh, there's **another fish**!" Label the object when she is totally focused on it—as she uncovers it.

3. Two toys and four buckets: Play this game as you have the others in this activity, but leave some buckets empty so you can talk about nonexistent things, too. If the child finds an empty bucket, say something such as, "Uh oh, **no fish**!" in a clearly disappointed tone with a sad face. Shake your head to indicate no, so she can learn the link between the gesture and the word. Go through the buckets, labeling and playing with the toys as long as she is having fun.

How do I know what the baby's babbles mean?

Interpreting the baby's babbles is difficult because her articulation is shaky. Follow her lead, and label the thing she is attending to rather than offering a word that sounds like her babble. For example, if she looks at a bottle and says, "Be," it is more likely that she means *bottle* rather than *baby*.

VARIATION:

When the child is a bit older, you can make this into a memory game. Label two toys, hide each under a bucket, and then ask for one: "Where is the **car**?" Can she remember where it is?

WHAT TO LOOK FOR:

○ Does the baby search for hidden toys?
○ Does she understand questions such as, "Where is the ___?" and start to look for the object?
○ Does she understand gestures, such as head shaking for *no* or waving for *goodbye*?
○ Does she babble when she plays with toys?
○ Does she understand a few words?

The Second Year: From Saying First Words to Combining Words

The second year comes with whopping changes all around as a baby becomes a toddler. He thinks, moves, and plays differently; he has better memory skills. By now, he is very good at following your gaze and gestures. He also enjoys quizzing you, pointing (often incessantly) at pictures and waiting for you to supply him with names for the objects in them. Your communication with him changes dramatically because his language progresses in leaps and bounds. By having attentive, language-rich conversations with him, you can continue to help him build vocabulary and become a more efficient listener and talker.

The most exciting event during this age is probably when the child says his first recognizable word. A toddler adds new words very slowly at first, but in the second half of the second year, word learning and talking take off. Sometime around sixteen to twenty-two months, many toddlers go through a vocabulary spurt when it will be hard for parents to keep track of how many words they say. A toddler learns new words more easily, even by overhearing speech from others, and he understands familiar words much more efficiently. Just as in adults, the left side of his brain now does most of the language processing. He works hard at articulating words more clearly and learns new kinds of words. Words show up for properties (such as color or size), locations, quantities, and feelings. Having more words overall gives a toddler more power to do something with them: He combines words to make his first sentences, and the first use of grammar appears.

Also during this time, a toddler takes his first steps into pretend play, much of it self-directed. He pretends to drink, to be tired, or to make a phone call. He needs you to engage in pretend play with him. By the end of his second year, this kind of play will no longer be just self-directed; he will pretend to feed his stuffed animals and dolls as well as himself. He may start to break down routines into smaller steps and act them out. He also is more aware of feelings and shows the first signs of empathy. He makes big strides in defining himself during this period and becomes concerned about his possessions, desires, and accomplishments.

Twelve Months and Up—Saying Real Words and First Make-Believe

5

Science Peek

Language researchers Daniel Swingley and Richard Aslin wanted to find out what toddlers know about familiar words. Fourteen-month-old children were shown pictures on a screen. Sometimes the screen showed an apple and a car; other times, a baby and a dog. A friendly, invisible voice asked each child to find one of the two things on the screen: "Where is the apple?" or "Where is the baby?" Sometimes, the voice mispronounced the names, saying, "Where is the opple?" or "Where is the vaby?" Did the children really notice if a familiar word was said incorrectly, such as opple *instead of* apple*?*

It turns out that they did notice. Those mispronunciations made it harder for the children to understand what was said and to find the correct image on the screen. A change in one sound threw them off, which means that even though toddlers often mispronounce words as they try to say them, they have very good memories of familiar words. A toddler needs you to say words correctly, so she can learn to say them and to combine them to form sentences.

Neil is fifteen months old. He loves picture books and cannot stop quizzing his mother. He speeds through the book, flipping pages quickly and squealing, "What'sat? What'sat? 'Sat?" His mother patiently answers, "A bunny. This is a kitty. A car, a VW Beetle. Wait, there is a blue ship!" But Neil is in a hurry and rarely waits for his mother's answers. Instead, he keeps asking, "What'sat? 'Sat?" while feverishly pointing at pictures. Then he switches his approach and decides to answer his mother's questions. He gets the first picture right, trumpeting out *be* (his word for *bunny*). His mother praises him and elaborates, saying "Yes, Neil. That is a bunny. A bunny hops!" When asking about pictures, Neil has decided to call everything a "be," regardless of what he is pointing at.

Neil enjoys his newfound skill in directing the conversation with words and pointing, and his behavior is appropriate for this age. Children Neil's age have pointing and asking down, and they enjoy initiating conversations. When reading with an adult, they often are not interested in exactly what the adult says but just that she responds with words.

Probably the most exciting milestone at this age is when a child says his first recognizable word, but communication and language advance in a lot of other ways, too. A toddler understands and imitates his caregiver's words and actions better, initiates conversations and familiar games more often, and begins to play make-believe.

Saying First Recognizable Words

A toddler's first real word is likely to be music to your ears! Saying a real word is a major language milestone and means that the child is on track to develop a spoken vocabulary. It is often difficult to decipher first words because they are embedded in lots of babbling. The words often do not resemble their targets: sounds can be simplified or left out. Toddlers often duplicate syllables (such as saying *nunu* instead of *noodles*) or leave out unstressed syllables (saying *nana* for *banana*). It is important that you respond to these simplified versions of words by modeling the correct word; do not reinforce the error by repeating the child's simplified version. Toddlers learn to say words best when they hear you articulate them correctly, clearly, and distinctly.

Characteristics of Toddlers' First Spoken Words

The first spoken words are those that are important to a toddler. They often include names of people he loves; names of his favorite toys; words for things that move, such as *ball* or *car*; names for animals, such as *dog* or *cat*; social words, such as *hi* and *bye*; and words describing events or things such as *up, more, no,* and *all gone.* Squealing *oh* when surprised, *there* to announce success, or *uh-oh* to declare failure are common as well. Early vocabularies tend to have more object names than action, property, or grammatical words.

The words can have multiple meanings for the toddler. For example, a single word such as *Da* may refer to *Daddy* or the car; it may mean, "There is a dog," when pointing at a dog; or it may be a generic request for your attention. One word often has a slew of meanings, simply because a toddler does not have the necessary articulation and language skills to express all of these nuances. The more he hears you clearly enunciate words, the more he can analyze sounds and work on his own words. Because first words require a lot of effort from the toddler, a new word may appear in his vocabulary only every few weeks. Words may even disappear for days, weeks, or even months, and then return suddenly, usually more clearly enunciated. Such fluctuations are perfectly normal as long as the child's spoken vocabulary increases over time.

Some toddlers talk earlier, some later, and differences grow quickly. According to the MacArthur-Bates Communicative Development Inventory (CDI) parent reports, there is little variation in how many words twelve-month-old toddlers say. The picture is very different at eighteen months, however: On average, eighteen-month-old toddlers say about 150 fifty words, with some saying no words and others a whopping 250. A difference of 250 words is enormous at this age and, while some differences may be explained genetically, others are likely due to the different language environments the children grow up in.

For example, Nereyda Hurtado and colleagues found that when mothers engaged and talked more with their eighteen-month-old children, by age two, their children knew more words and recognized familiar words faster than their peers with more taciturn mothers. But, it is not all about talking. Simple things in the toddler years, such as sharing attention, pointing, and looking at an object when talking about it, boost language learning and give children an advantage when they enter kindergarten.

Saying More Words at an Early Age Matters

Having more words in the vocabulary at an early age allows the child to combine words earlier, which is the first step into grammar. Children start to combine words when they have a spoken vocabulary of fifty to two hundred words. This may happen before eighteen months for precocious talkers, but for most children it happens later. Two other indicators that a child may start to combine words soon are when he imitates single words often and combines a gesture with a single word—for example, uttering *di* ("drink") while pointing at a dog drinking. Combining words is a big developmental milestone because children need to have sufficient motor skills to say a longer utterance and sufficient knowledge of words to relate two words.

Having more words in the vocabulary at an early age gives a child a long-term advantage in developing emotional skills. Research shows that children who have good language skills at two years old handle frustrating situations better at age four than their peers with less advanced language skills. Good expressive skills allow the child to use language as an important outlet to ask caregivers for support in challenging situations and to distract himself with words when he becomes angry.

Understanding More and Generalizing Words

A toddler likely understands questions and phrases, and when you ask, "Where is the ___," he goes into search mode. Or, when you say, "Let's go and get ___," he may get up and follow you, understanding that it is time to move even if he is still puzzled about why. He understands simple requests, and though he may not always arrive with the right thing, it is the understanding of the function of requests and questions that counts. Over time, he will understand more specific questions and requests. For example, he will point at his own nose instead of yours when asked, "Where is Luke's nose?" This is a good time to play games with simple requests and questions so he can learn the meaning of common phrases and object names. Also, at this age, a toddler's words are no longer bound to just one particular thing. While, earlier, the word *horse* only referred to the horse in his animal book, the meaning is now generalized to his toy horse and the horse he saw on a farm.

Sometime around a child's first birthday, another type of understanding develops. The child likely checks in with you in uncertain situations, such as when he receives a new toy. It is as if he is asking, "What do you think? Is it safe for me to play with?" This is called *social referencing*. If your face and voice are positive and enthusiastic, he will go ahead and study a new toy. If you look troubled and sound negative, he likely will back off. Understanding emotional and social expressions in voices and faces helps a child to navigate the world around him.

Understanding Varies among Children

Toddlers vary in how many words they understand, and individual differences can be quite big even at this young age. For example, one-year-olds understand around eighty-five words on average, with some understanding about twenty-five and others understanding around one hundred fifty. A difference of more than 100 words is gigantic at this young age, especially because toddlers understand so few words overall.

Keep in mind that toddlers understand more than they can say at this age. There is a big difference between *understanding* words and *saying* them. Examining individual differences in language learning, Elizabeth Bates and her colleagues found that it is perfectly normal for a child to understand two hundred or more words but only say one or two words. Comprehension often is ahead of expressive language by several months.

Starting to Point

The child's ability to point is a key engine for word learning. The toddler points at a thing and wants ou to engage with him. If you label the thing he is pointing at, he can connect the picture with the label. Consistently answering and labeling when a child points to objects and pictures over and over again is one of the best ways to jump-start word learning. The key is to label an object as the child is focused on it. Your answers give the toddler a feeling of being efficient, of getting things done: "I point, you label! And if you do not, I will keep following you around until you do!"

Pointing is a great way to expand conversations and make them more nuanced and specific because toddlers often point at very specific things—at the wheels or windshield wiper of a car, for example. In doing so, they hear and learn specific names of things. Being able to point himself gives the child the chance to quiz you and to learn more—provided that you respond to his curiosity and label the things he points at.

Make-Believe Play Begins

Have you noticed that your toddler pretends to do things? Maybe he picks up a toy phone, holds it to his ear, and starts a conversation; or he pretends to drink, then holds out the cup to his bear's face. This is make-believe, also called *symbolic play*. Make-believe play and language are tightly connected: They both require toddlers to think and use symbols. This is why babies with language delays are often encouraged to engage in make-believe play. A toddler's make-believe play will grow with age, but right now it is at the beginning stage called *self-directed pretend play*. The child pretends to do something with an object—for example, he pretends to talk on his toy phone. He also may extend familiar actions to other objects, such as putting his teddy bear to sleep by covering it with a blanket. The key is that you model pretend play.

Learning about the Functions of Objects

A toddler learns about objects by studying you. At first, he is a conservative learner. He uses the tool on the same subject as you do, and he does the action together with you—for example, he brushes the lion's mane as you brush the lion's mane. Later, he will be more adventurous and use the brush on all kinds of heads, even without you modeling the action directly. He has learned *deferred imitation*—imitating actions from memory. That is a big cognitive step forward because he can now pull out memories of actions and do them whenever he wants.

To foster a toddler's learning, show him what to do with all kinds of objects as you narrate what you are doing. Give him an identical tool so he can feed his bears with his own spoon or chat on his own phone. Even though a toddler will not understand everything you say, he will learn what to do with the objects and that they have specific functions. Comment on the child's object play just as you would on his gestures or words by giving affirmations and describing and labeling what he is doing.

Sorting and Linking Objects to Families Begins

Since children this age love studying objects, this is the perfect time to compare objects of the same family and contrast objects from different families. Sorting activities can provide lots of language practice as you help the child label items and you point out how certain things have something in common and others do not. Realizing that objects go together because of shared properties is a necessary skill for sorting. Although children this age are generally better at sorting things that look the same (all cars versus all plates), they will begin to sort items that share a common function, such as distinguishing kitchen things (cup, plate, spoon) from bathroom things (toothbrush, comb, and soap).

Toddlers start to sort mixed-up things in different piles just around the time their naming skills take off, around eighteen months; they seem to have an epiphany that everything has a name and belongs in a category. What and how toddlers learn about objects and their associated families depends on how you play and talk with them—for example, when you sort animals in one big family and vehicles in another, you can show toddlers that like things have common features: Trucks and cars both have wheels and go *vroom vroom*. Animals have legs and eat food. You foster learning by talking about and highlighting similarities of objects in categories.

Testing You: Stay Positive in Your Message

Toddlers have pretty strong minds of their own. Their determination, interest in exploring, and increased mobility is the perfect combination to get them into trouble, and you will need to start disciplining. Positive discipline has benefits for a child's social, emotional, and language skills. Toddlers actually do better when they have clear, consistent guidelines and boundaries, because they know what your expectations are.

How can you stay positive? Give toddlers options when they are about to do something dangerous or inappropriate, and redirect their focus—for example, "Your plate is not for throwing. Let's throw the ball together instead!" Look for an alternate activity to carry out; stay calm; be physically gentle; and use a loving tone, smiles, and positive words to encourage and support a child's accomplishments.

Positive Discipline Fosters Language Learning

In a 1995 study of more than forty families, Hart and Risley found that children whose parents used positive discipline strategies from age one year onward had bigger vocabularies and higher IQs by age three than those of parents who used less positive strategies. To illustrate how positive discipline affects language learning, imagine the following scenario: A toddler pushes over a cup of coffee, spilling it all over the floor. One mom reacts by saying, "No! Don't do that! Bad girl!" Another mom says in a calm, friendly, but firm voice, "Oh no, you spilled coffee! I don't like it when you push the cup off the table. It makes a big mess, and I don't like that mess. See, take the block instead—you can push the block off the table. That is not messy."

The key differences in these discipline strategies are the number of words, the overall tones, and the messages that they send. In the first case, the negative tone and words end the conversation abruptly. The explanations, comments, and redirection of the second mother may seem way over the head of her child, but toddlers do listen, infer from your face and voice, and learn from your words. Even though it is generally best to use shorter explanations at this age, children will learn from longer ones as well. A positive tone encourages the child to stay in the conversation, which allows for more learning. Too many commands and negative words cut conversations short and, over time, will make a toddler less inclined to engage with adults, resulting in fewer chances to learn.

Positive discipline takes work, time, effort, and carefully chosen words; however, if you offer a child choices; give explanations for why you do not like something or why something is necessary; introduce polite words such as *thank you, please,* and *excuse me;* and practice polite behavior, you will see real benefits down the road. He will be a more positive messenger and will regulate his emotions better, and you will have happier and longer conversations.

The Effects of Screen Time on Language Learning

The American Academy of Pediatrics recommends no television time or video viewing before age two. Infants and toddlers learn best in interactions with real, loving, attentive people. They thrive with tuned-in, interested people who play and talk with them.

Research has shown that too much TV slows language learning—for example, Zimmerman and colleagues found that for every hour infants spent watching videos, they learned six to eight fewer new words than those who interacted with attentive, live people instead. Infants between eight and sixteen months old suffered the most, exactly the age when every single word they learn really counts. Learning six to eight fewer words may not seem like much, but it actually is a huge deficit at this age, given that infants' vocabularies are very small overall. Screen time does not give children the necessary social and visual cues that they need to learn language.

The more the TV is on, the worse the quality of the conversations with and for toddlers. They spend more time alone, experience longer periods of silence, vocalize less, and have less to learn from. Parents spoke a stunning 770 fewer words with their children for every hour the TV was on, according to a 2009 study by Dimitri Christakis and colleagues. Fewer words spoken means fewer words heard and fewer opportunities for a child to learn.

Further, what is background noise for you is more than background noise for a young language learner. Because young word learners are much more susceptible to noise, the audible TV—even when in the background—makes listening and learning more difficult. As a result, he cannot pull out words or build word memories and word meanings as easily. Consequently, understanding and learning suffer.

First Spoken Words

Write down the date and circumstances of a toddler's first use of words. You can make columns for names of people, toys, animals, vehicles, body parts, food and drinks, clothes, action words, and descriptive words such as *all gone, hot, nice,* and so forth. The diary will be a valuable gift for the child later on, as well as a treasure trove full of fun and loving memories for you.

Language Checklist 5: Twelve Months and Up

Does the child	Often	Sometimes	Never
babble, combining two or more syllables, such as *da dada* or *da ka di kopʊ*?			
vocalize without moving his arms and legs?			
say at least one or more recognizable words?			
manipulate objects and explore how they fit together?			
play with more than one object at a time?			
understand simple directions, such as, "Bring me the doll"?			
identify familiar objects from a group of other things when asked, for example, "Where is the car?"			
follow your gaze and point to objects close by as well as far away?			
ask questions through words and babbles or by pointing while babbling?			
attempt to sort things?			
play pretend?			
initiate turn-taking games such as peekaboo, give and take, or filling and dumping? stay in a game with you for one to two minutes?			
point at things to engage your attention or ask for things?			
seek your face and voice in ambiguous or new situations, using your cues to guide his behavior?			
combine two words?			
say a variety of consonants?			
know how to use familiar objects appropriately, such as what to do with a spoon or cup?			

Communication Tips

○ Be selective in how you respond. Respond to words and speech sounds.

○ Respond to the child's gestures by pointing and elaborating on whatever the child points at.

○ Model words correctly; for example, if a toddler says *nunu,* repeat for him, "Yes, these are noodles."

○ Keep using baby talk, stressing important words and speaking clearly.

○ Repeat words often, and label objects when the child is focused on them.

○ Model pretend play. Have a tea party, put animals to bed, and so forth.

○ Expand single-word utterances to simple, full sentences—for example, if the child says *ba,* say, "Yes, that is a ball. It is a big red ball!"

○ Talk about and compare objects, and link them to families. Label each one and describe its appearance, color, size, and function.

○ Show and expand familiar actions to new subjects. Brush your hair, the toddler's hair, the lion's, and so on. This helps toddlers learn to generalize actions.

○ Act and narrate what you are doing at the same time, and give the toddler his own tools (brushes, spoons, and so on).

○ Copy the child's actions, and comment on them just as you would on his words and gestures—for example, "Oh, you are brushing the doll's hair!"

○ Ask questions using simple sentences; yes-no questions; and questions that ask who, what, when, or where.

○ Talk about memorable past events, using family or child care pictures.

○ Use simple sentence frames and stock phrases to ask, request, or direct:
  ○ Let's go ___.
  ○ Where is the ___?
  ○ Bring me the ___.
  ○ Do ___.
  ○ Don't ___.

○ Sing songs that use simple actions toddlers can copy. Include familiar nursery rhymes and songs that you personalize.

○ Read sturdy books with bright illustrations of everyday objects and events. Once a toddler knows some basic words, go into specifics.

○ Introduce story books about familiar routines, and create family books about routines and past events.

○ Avoid books with many words for now. Good books include those with simple songs, repetitive words and phrases, and rhymes; touch-and-feel books; pop-up books; and books about easily imitated actions, such as clapping, eating, dancing, and sleeping.

Copy Me, Copy You!

Toddlers usually love to copy an adult. A toddler best learns about action and object words by doing things with you, such as putting on hats, drinking from sippy cups, and so on. You can support word learning by encouraging him to imitate you and by describing actions and objects you both focus on as you play together.

GOALS:

- ❍ Talk with the child about actions, objects, and the function of things.
- ❍ Allow him to imitate your actions, and copy his actions and gestures.
- ❍ Foster understanding of action words and object names.
- ❍ Illustrate the association of specific actions with specific objects.
- ❍ Label actions or objects as you play with him.

SKILLS FOSTERED:

- ❍ Imitation
- ❍ Visual skills
- ❍ Understanding
- ❍ Gross and fine motor skills

MATERIALS:

2 hats

2 pairs of sunglasses

2 cups

2 spoons

2 buckets

Toys

WHAT TO DO:

1. Show familiar actions, label and talk about actions and objects, and encourage the child to copy what you do.

   ❍ Putting on hats and sunglasses: You each put on hats or sunglasses, and then take them off. Describe the action as you or the toddler is doing it: "**Look,** Tommy! I'm putting the **hat on**. Do you want to put your **hat on**?" Repeat this activity a few times. Trade hats and sunglasses to make it more fun. He can also learn about size this way when he discovers that adult hats and sunglasses are hard to keep on because they are bigger.

   ❍ Drinking from cups and eating with spoons: "I'm **drinking**. Do you want to **drink** something, too? Here's your **cup**!" See if the toddler copies you. Comment, "Good job! Now, we're both **drinking.** Mommy is **drinking** from a **cup**. Dylan is **drinking** from a **cup**." Or, eat together: Put a piece of cereal on your spoon, and say, "Look! I'm **eating**. Do you want to **eat**? Let's put a piece of cereal on your spoon and then you can **eat**, too." Take turns feeding each other.

   ❍ Brushing teeth: Hold a toothbrush, and give the child another one. Start brushing your teeth. See if the toddler copies you.

2. Repeat these activities with the same objects and new ones: Put hats on a toy dog, give the giraffe and the pig a drink, and so forth. This helps toddlers generalize actions.

3. Do silly things. Pretend to eat with a shoe, and see if the toddler is puzzled. If so, he knows that it is not quite right.

4. Reverse the game and copy anything the toddler does or says. If he plays with something, imitate exactly what he does with the object. Copy his gestures and words, as well. At the beginning of the second year, toddlers realize when they are being copied, and they love it.

Why should I imitate my toddler?

Your imitations tell the toddler that he is doing something special because the adult is now doing the same thing. He feels validated because he is now the leader. Researchers have found that adults who tune in to a child's explorations early on—by imitating actions, affirming that the child is doing a good job, describing and labeling actions and objects as the child works with them— help build conversations and language. Children who receive such feedback say first words sooner, reach fifty words sooner, and then start to combine words earlier than those of parents who are less responsive.

WHAT TO LOOK FOR:

❍ Does he copy your actions as you play together?
❍ Does he extend familiar actions to new things?
❍ Does he vocalize as he plays with things?
❍ Does he notice and enjoy when you copy him?

Repetition Counts: A Duck, Another Duck

Children who are just starting to learn words need to hear those words many times before they begin to understand what they mean. Repetition gives a child the necessary experience to gradually own and understand the word.

SKILLS FOSTERED:

○ Cognitive skills
○ Fine motor skills
○ Listening
○ Talking
○ Understanding
○ Visual discrimination

MATERIALS:

Box or bag
3–5 ducks in different colors and sizes (or other familiar toys of the same kind)

Preparation: Put all the ducks in the box or bag before you start.

GOALS:

○ Use repetition to help the child understand common words.
○ Connect an object name with different examples of the same kind to help him generalize names.
○ Use simple phrases in conversation to promote learning of grammar.
○ Label things often and consistently when the child plays with them.

WHAT TO DO:

1. Introduce the mystery bag or box, which is filled with ducks of different sizes and colors. Shake the box with the child to get his attention, then ask him what could be in it. Open the box together, pull out a duck, and close the box. Announce enthusiastically what you found: "**Oh, look**! What's this? It is a **duck**. Hello, big (or small or green) **duck**." Wave hello. Give the duck to the child and let him explore it as you talk about it.

2. When the child is no longer interested in that duck, pull out another duck and repeat the label several times as the duck comes out: "Oh, another **duck**! Hello, little **duck**. Now we have two **ducks**, a big **duck** and a little **duck**." Make each duck jump as you talk about it. Use simple, similar sentence frames as you label each duck to make it easier for the child to focus on the most important thing in the sentence, the object name. The goal is to have the child hear the label many times as he engages with the duck. Pause after you ask what the object is, and see how the child responds.

3. Once all the ducks have come out, play with them and talk about them. Pretend to feed, hug, and kiss them, brush their teeth, and so on.

4. After some time, put the ducks back into the bag or box. Pretend they are tired and need to go to bed. Kiss each duck, and say something such as, "Goodbye, **duck**. Good night, **duck**. Sleep tight, **duck**." Then observe what the child does as he puts each duck to bed.

WHAT TO LOOK FOR:

❍ Is he attentive as you label the object?

❍ Does he understand common words?

❍ Does he say first recognizable words?

Do I really need to say object names over and over again? It's boring.

What is boring for you is not boring for a child. Because word learning happens incrementally and is quite slow at the beginning, a child needs many repetitions to learn what an object name means. Repetition also helps in learning the sounds of the word and getting the sounds right, which is not an easy task at this age. Use object names in sentences, such as, "Here is the duck." This way, the child can learn how words are strung together. Simple sentence frames make it easier for children to understand familiar words. The more experience a child has with particular words, the more specialized the processing becomes in the young brain. Experience with language shapes the brain, and repetition gives more experience.

Where Is the Dog?

One-year-olds love it when things vanish and reappear. You can capitalize on this and foster understanding by creating a simple theater where familiar objects magically appear and disappear.

SKILLS FOSTERED:

- ❍ Cognitive skills
- ❍ Fine motor skills
- ❍ Listening
- ❍ Understanding
- ❍ Visual skills

GOALS:

- ❍ Talk to the child using baby talk.
- ❍ Help him to connect familiar sounds with familiar objects.
- ❍ Label objects in everyday play and routines using simple sentences.
- ❍ Comment on the child's correct responses through praise.
- ❍ Wiggle objects that you talk about to visually highlight them.
- ❍ Ask him simple questions that contain object names.
- ❍ Model pointing to the correct object.

MATERIALS:

A rope

A small white blanket or big towel

2–4 familiar objects, such as toy dogs, baby dolls, and shoes

Preparation: Tie the rope across two stable poles, and put the blanket over it.

WHAT TO DO:

1. Start by making the dog appear on the right while labeling it, "See, here's the **doooog**! Do you like him?" Make the dog jump around a bit then disappear. Put the doll out on the left and label it, "See, here's the **baabyyy**! Do you see it?" Make the baby doll wave and disappear. Repeat this a few times with each toy, switching their sides randomly.

2. Make the dog and the doll appear at the same time, one on each side. Ask, "Where is the **doooog**? Find the **doooog**." Wait for the child's response first, and then make the dog jump, and say something such as, "Here is the **doooog**! I'm the **doooog**!" Praise the child when he points to the right object.

3. The goal is to get the toddler to find the right object and, ideally, say its name and point to it. Go through the routine a few times, continuing to ask for both objects and switching their sides randomly. Use several different dogs and baby dolls—this will keep a toddler's attention longer and fosters generalization.

4. Introduce one new object, such as a shoe, and pair it with one of the other objects, such as the dog. Mix up your object pairs to see which words the child understands. Ask the toddler to identify shoes, dogs, or baby dolls. Always wiggle the correct object after the child responds, to attract attention to it and visually tell him which one is correct.

Emphasize Words

To help a child notice and learn a new word, emphasize it in the following ways:

❍ Make object names longer by stretching their vowels: **dooooog**.

❍ Say object names slowly.

❍ Stress object names by saying them a bit louder and putting them at the end of the sentence: Do you see the **dog**?

WHAT TO LOOK FOR:

❍ Does he identify some familiar objects correctly?

❍ Can he find objects when you ask for them?

❍ Does he show that he understands the function of questions by pointing, looking at the object, babbling, or saying a word?

❍ Does he say some recognizable words?

Does singsong, drawn-out speech really do any good?

Because toddlers' understanding is still fragile, when you give some extra help by using baby talk, you support understanding. Baby talk has many different jobs when it comes to language learning. At first, it gets a baby's attention and clearly shows him your affection. When the child starts making sense of speech, baby talk supports his understanding. Nineteen-month-olds understand familiar object names better when the words are stretched out and spoken slowly. Baby talk makes speech more intelligible for young word learners.

Families of Things: Animals and Vehicles

Language learning is not only about learning words for things. It is also about understanding relationships between things that have different names—for example, how are a thing called *pig* and a thing called *cat* alike? Grasping similarities among objects is important because it allows children to organize and to link objects to families.

SKILLS FOSTERED:
O Cognitive skills
O Listening
O Understanding
O Visual discrimination

MATERIALS:
2 shoeboxes
2 bags
3–4 familiar toy animals
3–4 familiar vehicles
1 unfamiliar toy animal
1 unfamiliar vehicle

Preparation: Put the animals in one bag and the vehicles in the other before you start. Set out the two shoeboxes.

GOALS:
O Label things with their object names (cookie) and their family name (food).
O Help the child learn new words.
O Link different objects to the same family.
O Play sorting games, describing similarities among things of a family.
O Label objects as you play.
O Help the child understand similarities among things of the same family by comparing objects that belong to the same family and talking about their similarities.

WHAT TO DO:

1. Take one animal out of the bag, label it, and describe its features—for example, say, "Look, a **pig**! I found a **pig**! Let's look at the **pig**. Oh, see these? What are these? These are **ears**. And these? Yes, those are its **legs**. I think the **pig** is hungry. Let's feed it."

2. Introduce another animal, label it, and compare the two, pointing out their common features and linking them to the same family name: "Yes, this is a **dog.** Where are the **dog's ears**? The **dog** has **ears**, and the **pig** has **ears**. Both **animals** have **ears**. The **dog** has **legs**. Where are the **pig's legs**? The **dog** and the **pig** live in the same house. This house is for **animals**." Indicate one of the shoeboxes. "The **pig** is an **animal.** The **dog** is an **animal**. Let's put them both there." Put both animals in the same shoebox.

3. Take one vehicle out of the bag, label it, and describe its features—for example, say, "I found a **car**! A blue **car**! Let's check out the **car**. It has **wheels.** The **car** goes **vroom vroom**. We can go for a **ride** in it."

4. Introduce another vehicle from the bag, such as a bus, and compare the two. Point out what a car and a bus have in common, then put the vehicles in the other shoebox, and say something such as, "This house is for **vehicles.** The **car** is a **vehicle**, and the **bus** is a **vehicle**. So let's put them together."

When you think the child has begun to understand the game, try the following activities. The point of this activity is not to learn all the words or family names. It is to begin to identify similarities among different objects and link them to the same family.

5. Take a familiar animal from the bag, such as a cat. Label and describe it. Ask, "Where does the **cat** go? Here with the **animals,** or here with the **vehicles**?" Explain where the cat should go: "The **cat** is an **animal**, so it goes with the other **animals**."

6. Observe how well the child can link familiar objects to the two families. Continue sorting other familiar animals and vehicles, following the same process.

7. Now take an unfamiliar animal from the bag, perhaps a zebra. Label and describe it for the child. Ask where it should go, and then explain, following the same structure as before.

8. Repeat the same process with an unfamiliar vehicle. Sorting unfamiliar objects is harder than sorting familiar objects because the child now has to observe and think about the characteristics of the object and group it with its family.

WHAT TO LOOK FOR:

○ Does he spontaneously sort things (regardless of whether he is correct)?

○ Does he sort things with you, and is he interested in doing so?

When does a child sort things?

Around one year of age, children may start to sort things into piles. They do so only sometimes and are usually far from correct. Around eighteen months, they may sort things without your help and often may do so correctly. Your words can guide the child to get the idea of sorting. Labels encourage children to compare things and to discover similarities among them. When playing, label an object before you ask your child to find the right family for it: "Where does the pig go?" rather than "Where does this go?"

A Present! What Is in Here?

One-year-olds love surprises. Unwrap the presents, one at a time, and encourage the *child* to say the names of the things he is unwrapping. Use familiar toys, and add a real present now and then.

GOALS:

❍ Encourage the child to say first words.

❍ Help him connect familiar sounds with familiar objects.

❍ Name everyday objects.

❍ Expand his vocalizations by confirming, describing, and asking questions—for example, when he says *da,* you say, "Yes, that is a **cup.** The **cup** has a flower on it. Where is another **cup**?"

❍ Model the correct words. When the child says *da* instead of *cup,* say *cup* clearly and slowly.

❍ Give him a feeling of being heard by responding to him, even if you are not sure what he is saying.

SKILLS FOSTERED:

❍ Fine motor skills

❍ Talking

❍ Understanding

MATERIALS:

Wrapping paper

Tape

Three to four shoeboxes, one for each toy (optional)

Three to four familiar toys, such as a shoe, duck, or ball

Preparation: Wrap each toy as if it is a gift.

WHAT TO DO:

1. Give the toddler the first present, saying something such as, "**Look, Will**! This is a present. Do you want to open it? Let's see what's in here." Have him open the present, and then ask, "What is it? Do you know?" Praise him if he says the name of the thing or babbles in reply—for example, if he says *de* for *duck,* model the correct word, "Yes! **Duck**. It is a **duck**. You are right!" If he does not respond, wiggle and label the object for him. Describe it and play with it together.

2. Continue with the other presents, following the same structure. If you have another object of the same kind, compare the two so the child can learn to link objects with the same name.

3. Once done, wrap up the presents with him, and start the guessing game all over again. Continue as long as he is having fun.

Note: Avoid making this game into a drill where you ask the child the name of the thing over and over again or even withhold the toy from him until he says something. This game is about having fun together. The child will say the correct name sooner or later.

Do I make it easier for a child to talk if I repeat his mispronounced words?

Since a toddler's first words most likely will fall short of the adult forms, it is best not to repeat them regardless of how cute they sound. You actually make word learning and talking harder by repeating his simplified words because you reinforce the wrong pronunciation. But, avoid overly correcting the child by saying things such as, "**No**, it is **not** a **da**. It is a **duck**. Say **duck. Duck.**" Keep the communication positive and respond to and expand on his vocalizations. Children need to hear words the way adults say them.

WHAT TO LOOK FOR:

❍ Does he have word forms for some objects (not the adult forms but some vocalizations)?

❍ Does he say a few recognizable words?

Pointing and Quizzing Other People

When you point at an object, you signal, "This is important. I am going to tell you about this so you can learn about it." The child is probably following your pointing already and starting to point at things himself. He realizes that his pointing pulls you into the conversation. If you label objects as the child points at them, this gives him the chance to learn new words.

SKILLS FOSTERED:

❍ Cognitive skills

❍ Fine motor skills

❍ Listening

❍ Understanding

MATERIALS:

Flashlight

Spatula

Stickers

Familiar toys

Preparation: Put stickers on a spatula to turn it into a magic wand.

Safety note: Never leave the child unattended with the flashlight or spatula.

GOALS:

❍ Show how to use pointing to engage other people, ask for things, and label objects.

❍ Introduce new words by pointing at specific things in objects, such as the wheels on the car or the tail of the dog.

❍ Help the child understand the function of questions.

❍ Respond quickly and consistently to a toddler's pointing by telling him about the thing or event he is interested in.

❍ Point to things with the child's help. For example, take his hand and touch his nose while asking, "What's this? It is your **nose**."

WHAT TO DO:

1. Start simple. Point at things close up, such as the objects in a picture book, while asking about them: "See, Luke. What's this? It is a **bunny**!" At first guide the child's finger gently and point with him at the picture. Connect pointing with a question; this way the child realizes that pointing is used to ask for something. Once the child follows you close up, point to things farther away, even outside, such as something outside the window.

2. Point at things using a flashlight. First examine the flashlight together, tell the child what it is, turn it on, and show how it works. In a darkened room, hold the flashlight together, shine its light on an object, and say something such as, "**Look,** Luke. See this? What is it? It is a **truck**." Let the object pop out visually just as you name it. You can also point at the object so that your finger and the light of the flashlight highlight the object. Have fun highlighting and talking about all kinds of objects, both familiar and new.

VARIATION:

Highlight objects using a magic wand to touch objects. When you touch an object with the wand, ask and label: "What's this? It is a ___." Always combine the pointing or touching with a question followed by the label.

WHAT TO LOOK FOR:
- ○ Does he point at things and babble?
- ○ Does he point at things, saying recognizable words for some objects?
- ○ Does he point at things while asking a question such as, "Wha' sat? That? This?"

Why should I respond to my toddler's pointing?

Pointing is a toddler's way of pulling you into conversation, asking for things he finds interesting, and communicating with you. The more reliably you answer, the more often he will point and ask. He will realize that you enjoy his curiosity and that he can rely on you to give answers. Pointing also gives a toddler the chance to be more specific long before he can say specific words. He can highlight one particular thing he is interested in, and you can tell him the specific name for that thing and beef up his vocabulary. The key advantage of the toddler's ability to point is that he gets you involved, gets to hear more of you, and he can then learn more.

Action Words

Toddlers are big doers and learn best by doing things themselves. He can learn a lot when he rolls a ball toward you while you say, "Yes, *rooooll* the *baaaall*." He learns what the action and the object are called; what action the word *roll* entails; and that this action and this object go together.

SKILLS FOSTERED:

- Cognitive skills
- Fine motor skills
- Imitation
- Talking
- Understanding

MATERIALS:

Balls
Doll
Plastic eggs
Stuffed animals
Toy figures

GOALS:

- Help the child understand action verbs.
- Help him generalize actions to multiple objects.
- Encourage him to imitate actions.
- Show and talk about what you can do with objects.
- Make action words visible by acting them out with the child.
- Talk about the relationships between actions and objects.

WHAT TO DO:

1. Use the ball and the doll to show familiar actions with familiar objects, and discuss what you typically do with them. Choose verbs that require simple actions, such as rolling, feeding, or eating. Say something such as, "See what the ball can do. It *rolls*. Let's *roll* the *ball*! Can you *roll* the *ball*?" Or, "The baby is hungry. How can we help? Let's *feed* the *baby*. Can you *feed* the *baby*?" By hearing the action word and the object name together while carrying out the action, the child learns to associate the two words over time.

2. Find out what the child has learned about the action word. Hold up the ball and the doll. Using the action word only, ask him to identify each one: "Which one can you *roll*? Do you know?" Or, "Which one can you *feed*? Can you show me?" Help if needed.

3. Introduce unfamiliar objects that go with familiar action words. Roll a football or plastic egg; feed the giraffe or the policeman, and so on. This helps a child to generalize the action across different objects.

WHAT TO LOOK FOR:

○ Does he understand some action words?

○ Does he extend familiar actions to other appropriate objects in play?

○ Does he copy actions he sees?

How can I help my child learn action words?

Toddlers understand some action words at around fifteen months of age—usually actions they can carry out themselves. Show and do actions with the child over and over again as you label the actions. Repeat them and stay close to the child as you show them, so he can better learn them. This form of engaging, called *infant-directed action*, gets young children's attention and helps them learn about objects.

Family Photo Book

This activity encourages the child to talk, identify people and actions, and think about past events. It fosters pointing, word learning, and memory. Read the family book regularly, discussing the pictures and asking the child to find particular pictures and pages. Avoid only asking questions—let him choose which pictures to discuss, and let him turn the pages.

SKILLS FOSTERED:

- ○ Imitation
- ○ Memory
- ○ Pointing
- ○ Social skills
- ○ Talking
- ○ Understanding

GOALS:

- ○ Give the child opportunities to learn about questions, objects, actions, and past events.
- ○ Let him practice turn taking.
- ○ Help him to understand the function of questions.
- ○ Ask yes-no and *wh-* questions that require more language. (What's the dog doing? Where is the truck going?)
- ○ Answer with and for the child to keep the conversation going.
- ○ Describe what interests him, in sentences, not just in single words.
- ○ Model correct words, and expand on the child's single-word utterances.
- ○ Read different kinds of books to him (touch-and-feel, lift-the-flap, and family books).
- ○ Ask questions and explain objects and events in pictures, including things he plays with.

MATERIALS:

Photos of the child, you, the rest of his family, or his pets doing familiar and special things, such as sleeping, reading, eating, cooking, or celebrating a holiday

Clear contact paper

Hole punch

Ribbon

Preparation: Cover the pictures with contact paper. Create a book by punching holes in the laminated photos and tying them together with ribbon. Include pictures of several people doing the same thing on one page—for example, mommy, daddy, puppy, and baby are all sleeping.

WHAT TO DO:

1. Ask questions:
   - about people—Who's that? Is that Grandma? Can you see/kiss Daddy? Where is Tommy?
   - about actions—What's mommy/daddy/the puppy doing? Are you sleeping?
   - about things—What are you eating/wearing/cooking/drinking? Do you like peaches? What is that? Is that a cup?

   The goal is not for the child to provide the right answers but for him to recognize that questions are to be answered. You ask, he responds, and vice versa. The more you model, the more the child learns, and soon he will initiate questions by pointing and saying words.

2. Describe and explain pictures. Descriptions provide lots of new language for a toddler to learn. Give details, talk about things using familiar and new words: "See, Daddy is **driving**. He is **driving** his big new **car**! It is a **red Beetle**!" Or, "Are you **eating** your **banana**? Do you like **bananas**? That is a pretty big **banana**." Start talking about the past: "See, you were at Grandma's house! Who else was there? Right, Daddy was there. He was outside with you. You went down the slide, remember?"

3. Link the pictures to real objects—for example, if you come across a picture of the child napping with his bunny, ask him to go and get his bunny. He will learn that words stand for objects pictured in the book *and* for the actual objects.

> **Why should I ask questions? He cannot answer yet.**
>
> Questions are a great way to engage a toddler's attention and to foster language learning, memory, and thinking skills. By asking questions, you help the child understand their function: to engage another person and obtain information. When you ask questions, model answering them yourself, at least at first. Asking questions early on has language and cognitive benefits down the road. Children of parents who ask questions early on refer to and talk about past events sooner and build better memories.

WHAT TO LOOK FOR:

- Does he respond to your questions with babbles, real words, or gestures?
- Does he ask you questions by pointing at something and saying words or phrases such as, "Da? What sat?"

First Make-Believe Play

Children love dolls, teddy bears, and so on. Use these toys to encourage make-believe play. Start with actions the toddler is familiar with from his own routines, such as hugging, kissing, feeding, diapering, and bathing. He will eventually extend the action to his doll, bear, or duck. The key is that he learns to generalize actions, which is a big cognitive step forward.

MATERIALS:

Dolls or stuffed animals

Props such as spoons, bottles, brushes, and cars

SKILLS FOSTERED:

- Cognitive skills
- Fine and gross motor skills
- Imitation
- Social skills
- Understanding

GOALS:

- Let him imitate familiar actions of others.
- Help him to understand object names and action words.
- Engage him in make-believe play.
- Model make-believe play and use lots of talk while acting together.
- Model actions the child has experienced and can act out himself.
- Integrate yourself fully by acting along with the child; describing; asking questions; and using gestures, sounds, self- and parallel-talk.

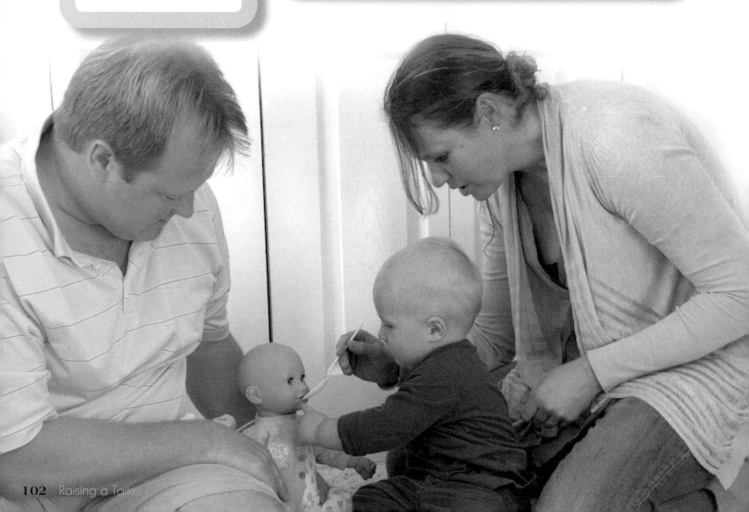

WHAT TO DO:

1. Start by showing a simple action while talking about it:
   - ○ "See, I am **kissing** the baby doll. Can you **kiss** the baby doll?" Point to the doll.
   - ○ "See, I am **hugging** the baby. Can you **hug** the baby?"
   - ○ "See, I am **rocking** the baby. Can you **rock** the baby?"

   Give the child the same prop and do the action together. Talk about what you are doing, so he can connect the action with its word. If he understands the game, see if he can hug or rock the baby doll without you modeling the behavior.

2. Act out routines the toddler is familiar with. Use real objects when you pretend to carry out actions:
   - ○ "The baby is **hungry**. Let's **feed** the baby." Pretend to feed the doll with a real spoon.
   - ○ "The baby's diaper is **dirty**. Let's **change the diaper**." Put a diaper on the doll.
   - ○ "Let's **brush** the baby's **hair**." Use a real brush on the doll.

   Talk about what the child is doing, and act with him. Give the play structure through lots language, descriptions, and questions. Avoid acting in silence—the purpose of your play is much less obvious then

3. Extend routines to other subjects—for example, feed all kinds of animals, not just the doll. This facilitates understanding by extracting the key features of the action: Feeding involves a spoon and a bottle and holding them to the mouth.

When can I start playing make-believe with a child? Why should I narrate our play?

You can begin playing make-believe with a baby around his first birthday, just as his word learning begins. When you narrate, your talk gives the play structure and encourages the baby to engage much longer. The sheer amount of talk he hears enhances language learning by giving him lots of experience with words and actions. Toddlers whose parents engage them in make-believe play early on develop better language, social, and self-regulation skills.

WHAT TO LOOK FOR:

- ○ Does he copy simple actions that you model?
- ○ Does he take turns and verbalize (babbles or real words)?
- ○ Does he extend actions to other things?

Eighteen Months and Up—Growing Vocabulary and Understanding

6

Science Peek

Eighteen-month-old Ashlyn is watching a movie. As pictures appear on the screen, she hears different sentences. Sometimes the sentences are correct, such as, "Where is the dog?" Other times, they are somewhat odd: "Where is ko dog?" or "Where is dog?" Ashlyn has a harder time finding the right picture when she hears made-up articles paired with familiar object names than she does when she hears the same sentence with the correct article. Sentences without an article are not any easier than those with correct articles.

Anne Fernald and I wondered what toddlers know about little words such as the articles *a, an*, and *the*. Many children that age do not say them, but do they hear them? Our study concluded that toddlers clearly attend to articles and use them when making sense of speech. Articles are crucial for learning grammar because they act like glue to bring structure to the words and hold them together. Talk to a toddler in full sentences with all the little words, because when you leave them out, you may actually make it harder for her to learn grammar.

The most visible and exciting changes at this age are probably that the toddler talks and imitates more and that you can understand her more easily. She combines words; first structures and grammar may appear in her speech. She also makes big strides in her thinking, memory, and emotional skills, and she figures things out in her head before doing them. She recognizes herself in the mirror, and make-believe play is in full swing.

Real-Life Story

Ethan, eighteen months old, held a spatula and stirred some imaginary food in a pan, uttering, "Cooking eggies 'patula. Tewa, tewa (stirring, stirring). More mik and four (flour), pease." I was blown away by his vocabulary and the way he used language to guide his play, documenting what he was doing and giving me directions.

Ethan is an incredibly sophisticated talker and thinker for his age. He combines more than two words in his sentences and uses grammatical endings (plural *s* on *eggies* and *ing* on the verbs *cooking* and *stirring*). His vocabulary is nuanced and specific; not many eighteen-month-olds say the words *(s)patula* or *stirring*. His pretend play is very structured, and he breaks down routines into little steps.

At this age, children make big strides in their vocabularies, and first structures appear in their speech. Generally, differences between children become bigger. Some talk in whole sentences; others say phrases.

Sometime closer to her second birthday, the child's feelings become more important and her interest in other people grows. All in all, it is time to take your conversations up a notch: Use more specific words, longer sentences, more open-ended questions, and have more diverse conversations, picking up on her interests.

Toddlers Learn New Words Quickly

A toddler now starts adding new words faster, and she learns them without you pointing things out directly to her. She no longer depends as much on joint attention and can assume the perspective of another, noticing where an adult's focus is, and can learn new words this way. She follows other people's conversations better and can pick up words by overhearing what is said around her. She makes very smart assumptions about new words—for example, when you look at the fruit basket and say, "Give me the papaya, not the banana, please," she will likely hand you the unfamiliar fruit. She quickly connects the unfamiliar word with the unfamiliar fruit. This is pretty skilled. Imagine just how many new words she can learn this way. She also learns new words while you sing songs or read books—words that you just mention on the fly and do not label directly. Although she learns words faster, she still needs for you to label and repeat new words, ideally in different contexts, to help her learn more about them.

Toddlers Interpret Familiar Words More Efficiently

By age two, toddlers interpret familiar words very much like adults, making quick decisions about what words mean as they hear simple sentences. Exploring fifteen- to twenty-four-month-olds' ability to understand spoken language, Anne Fernald and colleagues tracked children's eye movements as they looked at pictures while hearing familiar words. For example, the children saw a picture of a baby and a dog while hearing, "Where is the baby?" Although the younger toddlers needed to hear the entire word before orienting to the baby picture, the older ones did not. Two-year-olds zipped to the baby picture well *before* they even heard all of the word *baby.* This efficient understanding goes hand in hand with big changes in the brain. Around twenty months, a much more specialized brain has emerged. Certain regions in the left side of the brain are handling most language understanding, much like in adults.

It turns out, however, that not all toddlers are equally efficient processors. Some are better at quickly making sense of familiar words, and they seem to have advantages. According to Marchman and Fernald, toddlers who are particularly quick at interpreting familiar words at age two build vocabularies and grammar better over their second and third years and even do better in language and cognitive tests at age eight. The efficiency with which toddlers interpret spoken words early on has important implications for future success at school age.

Why are some toddlers more efficient in understanding speech? Although genes are a factor, the environment—your daily conversations and interactions—are most likely an even bigger driver.

Talking Grows at Different Rates

Toddlers may say a new word every other day. Once toddlers say somewhere between fifty and one hundred words, they go through a vocabulary spurt. This sudden explosion in naming can happen as early as fourteen months old or closer to the second birthday. Not all toddlers go through a spurt, however. Some add words more gradually. Either is normal.

Some toddlers are clearly on the fast track. Those children say about 260 words at eighteen months and about 550 at age two. Others take the slow road; they do not say any recognizable words at eighteen months and say about one hundred words by age two. Then, there are those in the middle; they say about one hundred words at eighteen months and about 320 by age two. These numbers show just how much normal development varies, and that individual differences are getting bigger during this age.

Keep a close eye on a child's progress if she seems to be on the slow track and does not yet say any recognizable words by eighteen months. Look out for potential warning signs (see Chapter 8), and consult a pediatrician if you are worried. Equally important: Do not let your conversations with a taciturn toddler slide. Instead, make an extra effort to tune in and tailor your conversations to the child's needs. There is some good news—if a toddler seems to be on the slow track at this age, it does not necessarily mean that there is a problem. According to research, the majority of late talkers with age-adequate nonverbal and comprehension skills catch up with their peers in vocabulary by the third or fourth year, and in grammar and discourse skills by school age. Nonetheless, extra vigilance and conscious efforts to converse and engage are important to help her to make up lost ground.

People often assume that boys are slower language learners than girls. Differences between boys and girls are actually smaller than what is usually believed, especially given the huge differences in normal development overall. Girls seem to be ahead of boys by about one month across the period from eight to thirty months, according to MacArthur-Bates CDI parental vocabulary measures.

Toddlers' Words Become More Specific

When a toddler has mastered basic words such as *ball, shoe, boat,* and so on, it is time to go beyond the basics when you label things. Twenty-two-month-old Neela did not approve of my basic choice of words and gave me a lesson in more nuanced words. When I asked, "Where is the ball?" she decisively corrected me, saying, "It is a **soccer** ball." When asked, "Where is the boat?" she said, "It is a **sail**boat." When she saw a Mini Cooper automobile, she happily squealed, "Look! A mini poopa!"

Generally, how specific and nuanced a toddler's vocabulary is depends on how specific and diverse your conversations with her are. Hearing more specific words from you gives her a chance to learn them and build a bigger vocabulary. Give specific names of objects she plays with—a tennis ball, a soccer ball, a VW Beetle, a spatula, and so forth. Talk about family groups, the color or size of something, or how an object relates to other things. She may not yet grasp all the explanations and details, but she will pick up what she can.

At this age, children start to talk about the properties of objects more often than before. She may tell you about the size of things or how they look, calling her baby doll a *big* or *pretty beebee;* your hands *dirty* or *messy.* Her car is not just a car, but a *bue da* (blue car), and the fish a *bet fis* (wet fish). She may also talk about feelings, count objects, and talk about quantities, and respond to *where* questions more specifically. She may state her possessions clearly, decisively saying, "My shoes," or simply *mine* as she grabs a toy from a peer.

Sometime between eighteen and twenty-four months, toddlers learn to understand and talk about quantities. Quantity can be expressed in different ways: number words such as *one* and *two;* quantifiers such as *more, some,* and *many;* or the plural, as in *shoes* and *dogs.* One of the earliest signs that children understand something about quantity is when they say phrases such as "more milk" when they want more of it or "more car" when they see many cars. At this age, plural words such as *shoes, hands,* and *socks* show up in children's speech, along with the first number words, even though toddlers do not yet fully understand their meaning.

Imitations and Word Combinations

At some point, a toddler sounds a bit like a parrot. She repeats many of your words and phrases. For example, if she picks up her toy keys, smiles, says "Goodbye," and walks to the door, you can ask, "Oh, are you going to work? Do you have your purse?" She may reply, "Go work. Got purse." Although some of the things a toddler says are copies of what you say, others are filtered through her own system and modified, such as when she says "no go" when you want to leave.

After having worked on single words for a while, many toddlers now combine words—usually once they have between fifty and two hundred words in their vocabulary. At first it may be tricky for you to hear the distinction between her single words and combinations. Listen carefully to the child's intonation. If it holds two words together, then she is combining words and not just piling them up one by one. When toddlers start to combine words, it seems that they have a specific construction plan. They use a few words such as *more, all gone, no,* or some object names and combine them with lots of other words. In doing so, they construct a sort of mini-grammar where an empty slot is filled with different words, such as in *more milk, more book,* or *more car; ball, baby,* or *shoe all gone; mommy, baby,* or *my shoe;* and *no go, no shoe,* or *no milk.* Over time, they will expand such short sentences by adding more words and grammatical endings. When a toddler starts to combine words depends more on her vocabulary size than her age, which is why building a solid vocabulary right from the beginning is so important. She needs to have a sufficient base of words before she can do something with them.

It is normal for a toddler to leave out certain words—for example, when kissing the teddy she may say, "Kiss teddy," or when giving the frog a bath, utter, "Wash woggy (froggy)." You will notice that she does not leave out words randomly. Little words such as articles (*the, a, an*), pronouns (*he, she*), and helping verbs (*is, are*) are missing. Every word costs a toddler energy and effort, so she first focuses on the important stuff: names of objects, people, actions, and properties. Toddlers can hear little, unstressed words, and they use them to learn about the underlying grammar. So, speak in full sentences and do not leave out the little words.

First Word Combinations and Sentences

Write down the date and the circumstances in which your toddler combines her first words. See if you can detect a pattern where she uses certain words in the same way: *bunny all gone, milk all gone; there bed, there bunny; more milk, more car;* and so on. Children's talk is systematic, so it may be fun for you to look for patterns.

First Grammatical Words and Endings

Some toddlers start sounding more like a grown-up at this age. They utter things such as, "This mommy's shoe!", "There's a tuwa (turtle)," or "Eating yummy waffu (waffle)." Grammatical words and endings make this talk different from a toddler's earlier versions. That is a big step forward, because grammatical words and endings are much more difficult to learn than object names and actions words. These words and endings are usually short, unstressed, and relatively empty in meaning. Among the first grammatical words are quantifiers (*more, another*), location words (*in, on*), pronouns (*me, I, that, this*), question words (*what*), and helping verbs (*is, are, can*). Among the first grammatical endings are *ing* additions to verbs, plural *s* to a few nouns, and possessive *'s* to state ownership. Even the past tense *ed* ending may show up occasionally. These tiny little words and endings make a child's talk much more precise and nuanced. They also indicate she is working on relationships between and within words. The words and endings usually show up once a toddler is well into combining words, which may be before age two for some toddlers or after for others.

Pronunciation Becomes More Intelligible

Around age two, about 50 to 75 percent of what a toddler says should be understandable—not just to you, but also to other people. However, mispronunciations are still common, even for the most precocious of talkers. You will still have to do quite a bit of guessing but far less so than several months ago. That said, keep the following in mind.

Although some words come out sounding the same, a child clearly knows that they mean different things. For example, when Maya pointed at a truck saying, "Thasa duck," I asked, "This is a duck?" She said, "No! A duck!" *Truck* is harder to say than *duck* because it has two consonants together: /tr/. At this age, it is quite normal for a child to simplify words, to leave out certain sounds or sound combinations, and substitute easier sounds for harder ones. /l/ and /r/ sounds often come out as /w/, as in *bwocwi (broccoli)*. She may also duplicate sounds in words (*goggie* or *doddie* instead of *dog*). It is easier to say two of the same sounds in a word than two different sounds. Also, some sounds show up fine in some words but not in others. She may say the /d/ in *daddy* but not in *dog*, which comes out as *gog*. How well a child pronounces single sounds depends on the other sounds in the word. Learning sounds is a bit-by-bit process, and modeling correct words is the best way to help a toddler learn to articulate words correctly.

Toddlers practice sounds and will do so during quiet times when they are alone—often in the crib before falling asleep or when waking up. They rehash words and memorable events and work on particular sounds. If you notice this kind of crib-talk, avoid interrupting her. Record her self-chats, if possible. The clarity of articulation may suffer in word combinations and longer sentences, at least for a short time. This is because stringing words together requires more tongue gymnastics and precision than saying one word at a time.

Make-Believe Play Becomes More Specific

Guide a child's make-believe play with comments and conversations, detailing the step-by-step actions that are involved in routines. For example, baking cookies includes preparing the dough, cutting out shapes, baking, and eating the cookies. Your language gives the play structure and provides the toddler with opportunities to learn more words.

Toddlers become increasingly savvy with props and routines; they likely will mimic what you do in great detail and keep track of the sequence of events. Toddlers extend and generalize new actions—for example, putting ointment not just on her own booboo but also on her doll's knee and the lion's leg. She describes what is going on: "Fis(h) is dwinki (drinking)," "I put lion bed," and "Lion tired." She may even act through her doll, such as when she makes the doll pet you or your family cat. She also uses substitutes instead of real objects, having phone calls on bananas or blocks, converting noodles into airplanes, and so forth.

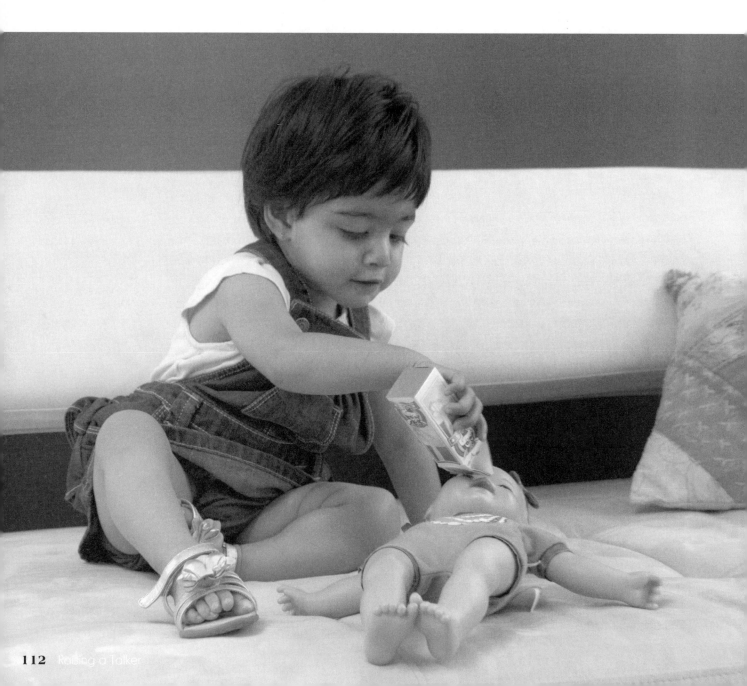

Toddlers Recognize Themselves and Use *I* Language

Sometime between eighteen and twenty-four months, toddlers recognize themselves in the mirror. They know that the cute face looking back is their own. Recognizing oneself is a big cognitive leap forward that usually brings along changes in language as well. Children who recognize themselves in the mirror use more personal pronouns (*mine, me, I*) than children who do not recognize themselves yet. It is as if knowing themselves opens the door for expressing their own needs, feelings, and actions. When a toddler discovers that she can refer to herself, she will experiment quite a bit, fluctuating among her name, *I*, and *me*. Self-recognition seems to push a toddler to define herself better, usually with I words—for example, saying, "I do da!" (I do that) when she has accomplished something or wants to do something; or "I sit," as she is sitting down. She tells you about her possessions, saying, "This my shoes" or just "Mine!" when a peer wants to take her toy. At this age, accomplishments, possessions, and ownership start to matter and will continue to do so well into the third year.

Around the time the toddler becomes more aware of herself, she also wants to understand you better—especially your reactions to something you do not approve of. She will carefully analyze your face and voice. For example, she will test the boundaries of *no:* does that word really mean *stop*, or is there some wiggle room?

Empathy First Emerges

Sometime around eighteen months or so, you will notice that the toddler becomes very interested in feelings—her own, yours, and those of other people. She will start to empathize with others—for example, when somebody is crying, she will want to help, giving advice or distracting the person who is upset. By age two, nearly all toddlers show concern if their parent or a stranger is in distress. She will ask, "What matter?" or bring you a cookie to make you feel better.

She may perform close body inspections and discover any potential booboos. She may bring you a bandage for your mole. She is starting to realize that her own feelings can be different from yours and those of others. This is a good time to engage in conversations about feelings. Give her the right language, so she can talk about her emotions. Recognizing her own feelings and being able to talk about them helps her to regulate her emotions better and fosters relationships with peers.

Using and Sorting Objects Improves

Toddlers now know very well what familiar objects are for. Cups are for drinking, hair brushes are for brushing hair, and so on. A toddler can show you the correct actions with the correct objects. When she learns a new name for an object, she quickly generalizes what it is used for. She also sorts things without your help and loves doing it. Play sorting games with her.

Language Checklist 6: Eighteen Months and Up

Does the child	Often	Sometimes	Never
say different consonant-vowel combinations?			
combine two or more words to make sentences?			
say at least ten words at the age of eighteen months?			
say at least fifty words by the age of twenty-four months?			
know the functions of objects and talk about what she does with them?			
imitate words when asked?			
understand three hundred words or more?			
understand complex directions, such as "Put the cup and the shoe in the box"?			
imitate a sequence of actions after a short delay?			
express interest in the feelings of others?			
understand if someone is in distress and show a desire to help?			
identify objects or events when asked?			
understand verbs in context, such as "The teddy is hungry. Give him something to eat"?			
use words to ask questions?			
sort things spontaneously by color, shape, and so on?			
show other-directed pretend play, such as feeding her stuffed animals?			
initiate turn-taking games, such as peekaboo or hide-and-seek?			
understand first property words, such as size and color words?			
recognize herself in the mirror and in photographs?			
add first grammar endings, such as plural s on nouns and ing on verbs?			
begin to refer to herself using her own name or words such as I, baby, and me?			
show signs of understanding quantity by using plural nouns and words such as more or another?			

Communication Tips

○ Model and expand the toddler's talk. If she says, "za fish," then you say, "That is right. It is a big fish!"

○ Use longer sentences and introduce new words paired with words the child already knows: "Give me the papaya, not the banana."

○ Point out relationships between words, such as a horse and a dog are both animals; the dog's paws are like your feet; or a flamingo is a kind of bird.

○ Model pretend play in more detail, and guide it with language. Break down routines into sequences, and narrate what is happening. Ask open-ended questions, give her props, and help her through the steps of familiar routines. Build upon her ideas rather than taking them over.

○ Use specific and diverse words. Talk about the color, size, and texture of objects. Give specific names and describe differences: "This is a soccer ball—it looks different from a football. A football is oval; a soccer ball is round." Give explanations, and inspect things in detail: "That is an ambulance. An ambulance is a kind of car. How many wheels does it have?"

○ Ask open-ended questions. Use labeling questions first, such as, "What's this?" or "What is she doing?" Once a child is a pro at those, start asking harder questions: "Where is the girl going?" "How do think the lion feels?" "Where can the boy hide the ball?"

○ Deliberately label and discuss feelings. Ask the child to imitate feelings she sees in others' faces.

○ Have mirror chats: Explore your faces or hands in a mirror, and talk about differences.

○ Offer choices to foster talking.

○ Match, categorize, and talk about differences and similarities of things. Link objects to families, and label the specific family members: a motorcycle, an ambulance, and a garbage truck are all vehicles.

○ Create songs to foster learning of new words and concepts.

○ Have daily book conversations. Read sturdy books with bright illustrations of everyday objects and events; large print; and simple stories that involve animals, familiar routines, locations of things, foods, feelings, colors, and so on. Use books with repetitive words and structures and a very clear story line.

Quack, Quack! Who Is That?

By now, your toddler knows quite well who or what makes certain sounds. While she listens to sounds and names of animals and objects, have her find the matching toys or pictures and answer your questions. To help her learn more than the sounds of animals, act out how they move, introducing action words and grammar: "Dogs can run fast. See, I am **running** like a dog." "I am **hopping** like a bunny."

GOALS:

○ Play listening games that require matching sounds with toys or pictures.

○ Use different kinds of sounds (live recordings, electronic sound files, and your own vocal imitations) for the same objects or animals to help her generalize sounds.

○ Introduce new sounds, animal names, and objects over time.

○ Act out movement verbs with the child and narrate what you are doing.

○ Let her imitate your actions.

SKILLS FOSTERED:

○ Cognitive skills

○ Gross motor skills

○ Listening

○ Talking

○ Understanding

MATERIALS:

Toys or pictures that go with certain sounds, such as a duck, bee, cat, phone, or dog.

Preparation: Make the sounds that go with the toys or pictures yourself, or record real sounds of barking dogs, roaring tigers, meowing cats, ringing phones, and so on. For animals, find sound files on the web at http://www.wavsource.com/animals/animals.htm.

Spread out familiar toy animals and other objects on the floor, or line them up in a row.

1. Make the sound of an animal or object, and encourage the child to name it. Start by making the noises of familiar animals and objects yourself. Say something such as, "**Listen**! I hear, I hear [pause] **roar, roar, roar.** Who says **roar**? It is a ___." Stop and let the child fill in the blank. Encourage her to find the matching toy and say its name. Help if needed and ask silly questions to engage her, such as "Does the fish say **roar**? Does the cow say **roar**?" Consider the following suggestions for sounds and objects:

   ❍ Meow—cat   ❍ Woof—dog   ❍ Roar—lion
   ❍ Choo, choo—train ❍ Vroom, vroom—car ❍ Buzz—bee
   ❍ Moo—cow   ❍ Quack—duck   ❍ Ring, ring—
   ❍ Baa—sheep   ❍ Tick tock—clock   phone

   Note: Bring variety to the game by using recorded sounds of different real dogs, trains, and so on, so she learns to generalize sounds across objects of the same kind. She will learn, for example, that dogs can sound quite different from each other.

2. Reverse the game, saying the animal or object name and asking the child to make its sound. Pick up the lion and say something such as, "The **lion** says ___." Wait and let the child fill in the blank. Show her the object so she has a visual, which makes the game easier and more fun. Help her if she does not know the sounds at first. Let her take over once she understands the game. Make mistakes such as, "The lion says **meow**." See if the child catches them.

3. Show and talk about how animals move, and introduce movement words. Ask, "How does a dog move?" Let her show you. Then say something such as, "A dog **runs.** Let's **run** like a dog. How about a bunny? A bunny **hops.** Let's **hop** like a bunny." Think of other animals that can run, hop, jump, and so on. Introduce new animal names over time. With more experience, the child will connect the movement words with the animals. Check her understanding by freezing mid-sentence: "Let's **swim** like a ___." See which animals she knows that swim.

Most children have built solid connections between objects and their matching sounds and matching words at some time in their second year. How well children build connections among sounds, words, and their corresponding objects depends on the experiences they have in their daily lives.

What if a child mostly says names of people and things?

All children do so at first because names for things are the easiest to learn. Names often refer to objects that the child plays with and adults often label: a book, a car, or a cup. She will soon fill her vocabulary with action and property words. Introduce such words now.

WHAT TO LOOK FOR:
❍ Does she match sounds with objects and animals?
❍ Does she say object and animal names?
❍ Can she complete sentences when you pause?

I See, I See a Flamingo

Encourage the child to find objects that you spy or that she spies and names herself. First, introduce the binoculars. Let the child look through them, and ask what she sees. If she does not respond, put your finger in front of the binoculars, wiggle it, and ask if she sees it.

Toddlers are fast comprehenders and can find pictures of familiar objects when hearing partial words only. They have good word memories that allow them to hear half a word and make a quick decision about what a familiar word could mean. However, children this age struggle to understand speech when words are muffled or less intelligible. Good clarity of speech is key for supporting toddlers' understanding.

GOALS:

○ Play listening games in which you ask the child to identify familiar and new objects using different object names.

○ Encourage her to imitate phrases and ask for objects.

○ Repeat sentences, using the same phrase and placing the object name at the end, to help the child learn how to say the sentence herself.

○ Introduce new words and objects when playing.

○ Expand your talk about familiar objects—discuss color, texture, size, and how objects relate to each other.

MATERIALS:

5–6 familiar toys
1 unfamiliar toy
Paper towel roll, cut in half
Glue
Colored paper

Preparation: Make a pair of binoculars: Glue colored paper on each half of the paper towel roll. Glue the rolls together. Line up five or six familiar objects in a row, or spread them out on a blanket.

SKILLS FOSTERED:

○ Auditory discrimination

○ Auditory memory

○ Fine motor skills

○ Talking

○ Understanding

WHAT TO DO:

1. Look through the binoculars and say, "I see, I see a… **baaaabyyy**!" Drag out the object word; say it louder to make it clearer. When the toddler finds the baby doll, praise her and talk about it. Then have her put it back or just continue finding objects. Continue playing as long as she has fun.

2. Ask for two familiar objects at once, which is harder because she has to keep two object names in memory. If she picks only one, is it the one you mentioned first or the one you mentioned second? Most likely, she will go for the second one because she heard that word more recently. If she gets only one, look through your binoculars and repeat your sentence.

3. Ask for very familiar objects using partial words, gradually saying more and more of the word: "I see, I see an **e**…, an **ele**…, an **elepha**…, an **elephan**…, an **elephant**!" Slowly unroll the word, giving her more and more of it before you say the full word. This fun twist gives you the chance to see whether the child can find an object before hearing all of the word. Use this strategy when you have object names that sound very different from each other and have two or more syllables.

4. Mix in an unfamiliar object whose name the child does not know. First ask for a few familiar things, and then ask for the unfamiliar one: "I see a **crab**. Can you find the **crab**?" Help and say, "No, **not** the ball, **not** the froggy." If she figures out that the new name has to go with the new object, celebrate! She has made a big step forward in learning new words quickly.

5. Reverse the game. Encourage her to say, "I see, I see ___ (object name)." The goal of this activity is that she names an object and then she herself gets it, or you can get it for her. Coach and whisper the phrase so she can memorize the sentence frame and say more than just the object name. You can also take turns in asking and getting things.

   Note: Start with a few objects and gradually add more. Once the child knows basic size or color words, include objects of different sizes and colors. Say the property words: I see, I see a **big**…**duck**. Deliberately pause after the property word, so she can rule out some items.

> **Is it okay if a child sometimes calls things with the wrong names or says only parts of words?**
>
> That is just fine at this age. So-called *overextensions*—such as calling a zebra a horse—will fade out over the next year. It is best to model the right word but not overly correct the child: "Oh, you mean the **zebra**?" Also, when saying words, toddlers often first say only the strong, stressed parts of words (*nana* in *banana*) and drop the unstressed. In the third year, words will become more complete because toddlers have better motor control.

WHAT TO LOOK FOR:

- ❍ Does she find objects you ask for when you say full words?
- ❍ Does she find objects before hearing the entire object name?
- ❍ Does she imitate and expand phrases? (Rough imitations count.)
- ❍ Does she find unfamiliar objects among familiar ones?

Picture Puzzles: Connecting Object Halves

This game fosters thinking and visual memory. Toddlers love puzzles, and these simple picture puzzles require some mental gymnastics. She sees only half of a familiar object and has to find the other half and then connect them.

Toddlers learn new words faster and more nimbly in the second half of their second year. They no longer depend as much on joint attention and can assume the perspective of others, noticing where an adult's focus is. Toddlers now have many ways to learn new words, which allow them to build their vocabularies more rapidly.

Why should I ask a toddler about halves of objects?

This activity makes her think and search the visual memories of objects stored in her brain. Her answers will give you great insights into how she thinks. Children notice the shape and color of things and may use these cues to guess what a half of an object could be.

GOALS:

○ Help the child connect object halves, guess objects from halves, and learn color words.

○ Talk and ask about specifics of familiar objects. Point out details to give her new things to learn and think about.

○ Model questions, such as *who, what,* and *where* questions and yes-or-no questions.

○ Ask her to identify familiar objects in everyday situations.

SKILLS FOSTERED:

○ Fine motor skills

○ Talking

○ Understanding

○ Visual discrimination

○ Visual memory

MATERIALS:

Magazines or catalogs

Scissors

Clear contact paper

Pictures of everyday objects

Preparation: Cut out pictures from magazines and catalogs. Cover them in contact paper, and cut each picture in half.

WHAT TO DO:

1. Spread out the cards on the floor. Mix them up. Pick up one object card (such as half a banana) and ask the child what it could be. See if she has suggestions, and then ask her to find the other half to connect the two. Go through the half pictures one by one, putting the banana half next to each card and asking if they go together. See if she can find the correct half herself. When she comes across the other half of the banana, show her how to connect the two and name the object: "It's a **banana**!"

2. Pick up another card, and ask what this object could be. Give the child some choices if she does not respond. Ask for implausible objects—for example, when you hold up half an apple, ask, "Is it a **truck**? Is it a **teddy bear**?" These questions will get her to think and talk, so do not give away the right object in your questions. Give her the card and let her find the correct match. Go through the other cards with her, one at a time, asking what each one could be. Deliberately make mistakes and put wrong cards together (half an apple with half a cup) and ask if that is right. Toddlers this age love to help, and this way she can shine as she corrects you.

3. Discuss colors and cues: "Which color is this? It is **yellow**. Can you find another card with **yellow**?" "What do you see on this card? Yes, these are **wheels**. Which thing has **wheels**? Let's look for a card that has **wheels** on it." The child may find halves but struggle with how to connect the two. Show her how to rotate the object cards to connect them to a whole. Children are very good at matching things for color or shape, but rotation is harder.

   Note: Start out simple with two or three object cards (four or six halves) of very familiar objects. Later, add more pictures, and make the game harder using objects of the same color or shape. Use object families such as animals, vehicles, or fruit. Add a new object whose name the child does not yet know. You can expand this game in many ways and play it for the whole next year.

WHAT TO LOOK FOR:

❍ Does she find the missing halves of familiar objects?

❍ Can she name the objects once the halves are connected?

❍ Has she started to combine words when talking?

❍ Does she answer yes-or-no questions appropriately?

❍ Does she guess what object halves could be?

Object and Action Words: Is the Cup for Digging?

A toddler knows a lot about actions and objects now. She knows that certain actions are done with certain tools—for example, you brush your hair with a hairbrush and drink with a cup. She also enjoys correcting you. Use a puppet to get the toddler engaged.

SKILLS FOSTERED:

❍ Fine motor skills

❍ Memory

❍ Talking

❍ Understanding

MATERIALS:

Tools, such as a hairbrush, toothbrush, cup, sock, and keys

Paper bag

Puppet

Preparation: Put the tools in a bag.

GOALS:

❍ Foster learning of grammar, including using -ing on verbs.

❍ Describe what the child is doing, and relate objects and actions.

❍ Give wrong names or action words, so the child can learn about negation: "This is **not** a cup. This is **not** for drinking."

❍ Model what objects are used for and narrate using self- and parallel-talk.

❍ Talk in full sentences including little words such as articles and pronouns.

❍ Make mistakes so the child can correct your actions and words.

WHAT TO DO:

1. Introduce the puppet, and tell the child that it has a bag full of things. Have the puppet pull out an object such as a hairbrush and ask, "What is this? Is it a **cup**?" If the child does not answer, model so she learns the game: **"No**, this is **not** a cup. (Shake your head.) It is a **brush**! A pink **brush.**" Pull out one object after another, always asking a silly question first, and see how she responds. The goal is that she corrects the puppet using negation and naming the object correctly. Use objects the child is very familiar with so she can enjoy correcting the puppet. Mix up naming things with the correct or wrong name.

2. Encourage the child to help the puppet find the right tool for what he wants to do. Have the puppet pull an object from his bag and say something such as, "Look! I found a **cup**! What's it for? For **brushing my hair**?" Wait for the child's answer, and then help her, "**No**, it is **not** for **brushing**. The **cup** is for **drinking**." Ask the child to give the puppet a drink. Pull out one object after another, and see if she can model the right kind of actions with the tool the puppet pulls out. The goal is that she models and says the correct action word. Stick to simple sentences

using the same structure, so she can learn it. Be silly, and model wrong things first. Here are some suggestions for play:

○ Pull out a sock, and pretend to put it on the puppet's head. Ask, "Where do **socks** go?" Wait for the child's response, and then expand, "Yes, **socks** go on **feet**. Let's put them on our (or the puppet's) **feet**."

○ Oh, look, a **key**. What's the **key** for? For **brushing** my teeth? No, for **opening** the **door** of a car or house.

○ Oh, look, a **phone**. What's it for? For **drinking**? No, for **calling** people.

○ Oh, look, a **toothbrush**. What's it for? For **brushing** my **feet**? No, it's for **brushing** your **teeth**.

○ Oh, a **pillow**. What's it for? For **eating**? No, for **sleeping**.

○ Oh, a **rattle**. What's it for? For **driving**? No, for **making music**.

○ Oh, a **shovel**. What's it for? For **making** a **phone call**? No, for **digging**.

○ Oh, a **spoon**. What's it for? For **cleaning** my **shoes**? No, for **eating**.

Note: Practice make-believe play, having the child give drinks with cups and bottles to all kinds of animals, unlocking all kinds of doors with keys, brushing all kinds of heads, and so on. This helps her learn to generalize meanings and extend make-believe play to others.

WHAT TO LOOK FOR:

○ Does she understand the function of objects and extend familiar actions to all kinds of subjects?

○ Does she correct you by filling in the right object names and action words?

What if my child only says some words and leaves out others?

Children this age often leave out little words and grammatical endings. Instead of saying, "I am eating the cookie," they say, "Eat cookie." Little words such as articles are harder to hear than object names or action words because they are short and unstressed. It is likely that toddlers do not say articles and other little words because they are not as helpful to them and because they generally carry much less meaning than object names and verbs. Little words are also difficult to say together with the big words, requiring a lot of motor control that the child does not quite have. Children focus on the big words but need to hear full sentences with all the little words and endings from you.

All about Me

Sometime between eighteen and twenty-four months, a toddler makes a huge cognitive leap forward and recognizes her own image in the mirror. When she looks at her reflection, she realizes, "It is me in there, not just any cute girl!" This self-recognition goes together with an emerging sense of self. She becomes much more aware of who she is, of her own looks, needs, desires, and feelings. Now is a good time to use pronouns such as *my, I,* and *mine* to help her define herself more clearly and precisely.

This child's favorite word is *mine*, everything is *mine*! Why?

With a stronger sense of self comes a strong sense of ownership. Interestingly, toddlers who quickly claim "mine" when grabbing a toy from a peer at eighteen months are actually better social players at twenty-four months. They smile more, play with their peers, and share toys. Presumably, the ability to talk about possessions—to set the ground rules about what's yours and what's mine—helps children get along better with peers in the long run.

GOALS:
- Help her understand how to talk about herself and others.
- Use pronouns to identify objects as you play sorting games with the child.
- Let her practice self-recognition.
- Model the connection between self-pointing and words such as *I* and *my* and the connection between pointing at others and words such as *you* and *your.*
- Use possessive pronouns with familiar object names to demonstrate differences in possession.
- Emphasize pronouns when you compare objects to help her understand what they mean and how they are used.
- Correct wrong uses by modeling the correct form but not overtly pointing out the mistake.
- Talk about possessions and relationships in your everyday conversations to help her become aware of these concepts.

MATERIALS:
Unbreakable mirror
2 baskets
Clothes and things that
   belong to you and the
   child
Stickers (optional)

SKILLS FOSTERED:
- Body awareness
- Cognitive skills
- Self-awareness
- Social-emotional skills
- Talking
- Understanding

WHAT TO DO:

1. Use an unbreakable mirror where you can see both of your faces and talk about your body parts using lots of pronouns.

    ○ Have the child copy and imitate you. The goal is that she learns to relate words such as *my* and *I* with herself. Point to your own nose, and say, "**My** nose!" Help the child to point at her own nose, and whisper what she should say: "**My** nose." Continue with other parts of the body, pointing and modeling what she should say. Model actions, point at yourself, and say, "**I** am waving. **I** am clapping." Have her point at herself, and coach her. She will learn that when she points at herself, it goes with words such as *my* and *I*.

    ○ Compare body parts, and contrast *my* and *your*—for example, touch your nose, and say, "This is **my** nose! This is **mommy's** nose! This nose is **mine**!" Then ask, "Where is **your** nose?" Point to her. "Show me **your** nose! Emma, is this **your** nose?" Touch her nose if she does not.

    ○ Without pointing, give directions such as, "Touch **my** nose." See if she understands you without the visual cue. If not, help by pointing. "Can you put a sticker on **my** nose? On **your** nose? Show me **your** ears." Have the child put stickers on the parts you ask for—many toddlers love stickers. Name very familiar body parts, so she can focus on the pronouns.

2. Put clothes and toys from both of you in one pile. Tell the child to sort by putting your things in one basket and her own things in the other. Discuss who something belongs to, to guide the play: "Emma, look what I found! Whose is this? This is **my** shirt!" Point to yourself. "It is **mine**! Can you find **your** shirt?" As she finds her T-shirt, coach and whisper, "You can say **my** shirt." Use things about which she feels very strongly to encourage talking. Keep sorting and discussing what belongs to whom.

3. Toddlers love to strut around in your things. Play a game with lots of pronoun talk. Ask for each other's clothes, and model: "Emma, can I wear **your** shoes? Point at her. "Do you think **your** shoes are going to fit? Uh-oh! **Your** shoes are too small for **my** feet." Point at yourself. "Do you want to try on **my** shoes?" Point to her, then to your shoes.

4. Find out if the child recognizes herself with a simple game. Put a dot of rouge or lipstick on the child's nose, distract her, play with her for a while, and then put a mirror in front of her. See how she reacts. If she wipes the red dot off or is embarrassed that she was running around with this red thing on her nose, then you know that she has mastered self-recognition.

WHAT TO LOOK FOR:

○ Does she talk about herself using different words such as her own name, *I*, and *me*?

○ Does she claim and talk about her own possessions?

○ Does she understand pronouns in requests: "Where is your nose?" "Where is my nose?"

○ Does she recognize herself in the mirror?

Color Words: Red Cars, Blue Cars

Toddlers love to play with cars or trucks and engage in activities that you do in your daily life. Talk about color words as you play with toy vehicles. Start simple, using only two colors at first.

GOALS:

❍ Pretend with her, and encourage her to match things for color while you play.

❍ Vary color words in your talk. Put the color word after—not just before—the familiar object name. When you say the color word after the object name, the child can first focus her attention on the familiar object and then learn something about its property.

❍ Help her understand color words by stressing them, especially when contrasting two objects.

❍ Discuss the color of identical objects so the child can focus on the similarity of both objects: "This cup is **red**. And, this cup is also **red**."

❍ Discuss the color of different objects to teach a child that a color is not bound to a particular thing and to help her generalize color across different objects: "The balloon is **red**, and the car is **red**."

❍ Help her understand negation: "This car is **not** blue."

❍ Read books that explore color families.

SKILLS FOSTERED:

❍ Cognitive skills
❍ Fine motor skills
❍ Talking
❍ Understanding
❍ Visual skills

MATERIALS:

5–6 toy vehicles of the same color
5–6 toy vehicles of a different color
Plastic squares or colored paper in the same colors as the vehicles

Preparation: Cut out colored squares (or use plastic ones) to use as gas stations and parking spaces.

WHAT TO DO:

1. Place two to four cars, in two colors, in front of the child. Describe them together. Ask for details such as where the doors and wheels are, what kind of noise they make, and so forth. Compare the cars and point out how some are the same in color: "Look, this car is **red**. Which other car is **red**?" Point out how others are different in color: "See, this car is **red**. That car is **not** red. That car is **blue**."

2. Spread out the color squares and pretend that they are gas stations. Drive around with the cars and suggest that the car is stuck and needs gas. Pretend to get gas at the squares that match the colors of the cars. Guide the play with color words: "The **red** car is out of gas. Let's drive the **red** car to the **red** gas station. See, there's the **red** gas station." Pretend to get gas for all the red cars, and then repeat the same activity for all the blue cars, using color words as you talk. Continue playing and prompting for color words: "My **blue** car is out of gas. Where should it go—to the **blue** gas station or to the **red** gas station?" Wait for an answer, and then guide the child: "Yes, **blue** cars go to the **blue** station."

3. Pretend you both need a break and want to park the cars. Pretend that the squares are now parking lots. Have the child park the cars in the matching parking spots and then go for lunch together. Guide the play using color words: "I need to park the **red** car. Where shall I park it—at the **red** spot or at the **blue** spot?" Provide lots of opportunities for color talk by parking a whole fleet of cars at the matching spots.

When can I expect a child to understand color words?

Children start to understand color words generally between two and three years old, but how quickly they understand color words likely depends on what kind of experiences they have had with those words. When you use color words, try to say them after the object names, as in, "The house is yellow." Saying the color word after the familiar object name seems to provide a learning boost, helping the child connect the color with the word being described.

WHAT TO LOOK FOR:

○ Does she find objects of the same color on her own?

○ Does she spontaneously match objects for color (all red things)?

○ Does she respond to color questions with any color word (does not need to be right)?

○ Does she understand one or more color words?

○ Does she say one or more color words?

Property Words: Big and Little Things

Once children have learned the names of things, they begin to focus on properties: big or little, squishy or hard, dirty or clean, and so on. Although this activity focuses on size words, the activities can be played with any contrasting property words.

SKILLS FOSTERED:

○ Cognitive skills
○ Fine motor skills
○ Gross motor skills
○ Talking
○ Understanding

GOALS:

○ Play matching and sorting games with her.
○ Contrast sizes in objects of the same kind: "This shirt is **little**. That shirt is **big**."
○ Emphasize property words in your speech to help her understand size words.
○ Ask questions to help her think about size: "Who is **little**— Mommy or you?"
○ Use pronouns in combination with property words to help her understand *my* versus *your*.

MATERIALS:

Familiar toys in two sizes
1 big basket or box
1 little basket or box
Masking tape or ribbon

Preparation: Make a big and a little square on the floor with masking tape or ribbon.

WHAT TO DO:

1. Spread out a few object pairs that differ in size.
   - ❍ Compare two objects of the same kind: "This is a **big** bottle! Can you find another bottle? There's a bottle. This bottle is **little**. This bottle is **not big**." Show the size difference and put the objects side by side. Contrast other objects, making sure the size difference between the two objects is clearly visible. Talk about the size difference, and let the child compare two objects that differ in size.
   - ❍ Put little things in a little basket and big things in a big basket. Ask questions such as, "Where do you think the **big** ball goes? In the **big** basket (point to it) or in the **little** basket (point to it)?" Explain, "Yes, the **big** ball goes in the **big** basket. The **little** ball goes into the **little** basket." Continue sorting until all the objects are in the right locations. To vary the game, pretend to be a baby and say that you need all the little things. Let your child pretend to be the mommy, and tell her she needs all the big things. Toddlers love to have big things.

2. Make one or two big squares and one or two little squares on the floor with masking tape or ribbon. Keep your directions simple, and do the actions with the child: "Let's run to the **big** square." Run with her to the big square. Come back to a designated starting point, and start over: "Let's run to the **little** square." Gradually let her find the correct square on her own, so you can see how well she understands the two size words. Mix up the size words randomly in your directions, so she has to really listen and not just jump from one square to the other. Over time, add another big square and little square. Once she knows the game, she can give you directions.

VARIATION:

To make the game harder, add a different shape such as a circle. She now has to listen to the size and shape words to find the right spot. To add even more variety, use new movement words such as *jumping, crawling, lying down.*

Which properties do children learn first?

Many children learn the word *hot* first, presumably because their parents warn them away from hot things for safety reasons. Words for shape are usually learned before color and texture words. What words and what age they say them depends on the child's experiences and the games and conversations they are engaged in. Generally, children learn a property best when comparing familiar things of the same kind, such as a big cup and a little cup. Property words that are accessible through the child's senses—*big, little, dirty*—are learned early. These properties are concrete: Children can see and touch their meanings.

WHAT TO LOOK FOR:

- ❍ Does she spontaneously sort things for properties?
- ❍ Does she understand some property words, such as *big*?
- ❍ Does she say some property words?

Spatial Words: Put the Monkey on the Bucket

Location words such as *in*, *on*, and *under* express where things are in relation to other things. Toddlers have had lots of experience moving things around—putting the apple *in* the pot, the duck *on* the table, and so on. It is around this age that they start to understand and say location words. This is the right time to talk about where things are.

GOALS:

○ Show, model, and contrast location words, using self-talk or parallel talk.

○ Give directions for the toddler to act out location words.

○ Play hide-and-seek games where you put objects in different locations and let the child find them.

○ Use blocks, figurines, and vehicles to show spatial concepts. Narrate what you are doing.

○ Read books, guide play, and ask questions using spatial words.

○ Guide her to understand and answer location questions such as, "Where is the duck?" or "Can you find the book?"

SKILLS FOSTERED:

○ Cognitive skills
○ Memory
○ Motor skills
○ Talking
○ Understanding

MATERIALS:

6 familiar toy animals
6 big buckets or boxes
2 bags

WHAT TO DO:

1. Place three toy animals in a bag. Place two buckets upside down and one standing upright. Pull an animal from the bag and say, "Hi **duck!** Where do you want to go?" Have the duck answer in a silly voice, "I want to sit **on** the bucket!" Ask the child, "Cora, can you make the duck sit **on** the bucket? Put the duck **on** the bucket, please." Help the child put the duck on the bucket, and then say something such as, "This duck is **on** the bucket!" Pull out the next toy, ask it where it wants to go, let it answer, and then say, "Cora, the giraffe wants to sit **under** the bucket. Put the giraffe **under** the bucket, please." Repeat this activity for *in*. Then relocate the animals, asking the child where she would like to put them. Give choices and guide the play with spatial words and talk, asking if she wants to put a toy duck *in, under,* or *on* the bucket.

2. Have three animals in a bag and three buckets for yourself, and the same for your child. Place four buckets upside-down and two standing up on the floor. Take out one animal and describe what you do, highlighting the spatial word: "I'm putting my duck **on** the bucket." Ask

the child copy you: "Can you put your duck **on** the bucket?" Help her if needed. Repeat this activity for *in* and *under*. Guide the play with lots of spatial words.

3. Encourage the child to find the animals that you hide. Show and label two animals: "Here's a **duck.** Here's a **frog.**" Have her close her eyes, and then hide the toys. Ask for one toy: "Where's the **duck**? Find the **duck**." Let her open her eyes and search for the toy you named. Guide her search with spatial words: "Is it **on** the bucket? No, the duck is **under** the bucket." She has to memorize the correct word as she searches for the object. Once she has found both toys, start over. Then, let her hide things for you to find.

4. Have the toddler move around as you give directions, or have her move one or two animals around. Give directions such as, sit *on* the chair, go *under* the table, sit *in* the box, and so on. Tell her to put the monkey *on* the truck, put the duck *in* the box, put the duck *under* the hat, and so on.

WHAT TO LOOK FOR:

○ Does she understand some location words, such as *in, on,* or *under*?

○ Does she say location words?

○ Does she understand location questions?

How does a toddler learn words for locations?

The first spatial words that children understand and say are *in, on,* and *under. In* is often the first because children have lots of experiences putting things in containers. *On* and *under* are most easily learned with surfaces such as tables, chairs, and beds. Many toddlers say *on* and *in* by age two; *under* is conceptually harder and is usually understood and spoken later. When a child understands and talks about locations depends on the experiences in her daily life. As you play, guide the child with language: "Let's put the car *in* the garage."

Feelings Words: Happy and Sad

Faces are important clues to our emotions, and toddlers are now becoming very interested in feelings, both theirs and those of others. Understanding feelings requires that a toddler recognize what indicates happy or sad. This is best learned by talking about expressions on faces.

GOALS:

- Show and talk about emotions on your own face, faces in books, and on toys.
- Help the child learn about emotions by describing what makes someone look happy or sad and by comparing and contrasting feelings with pictures that show emotions clearly.
- Play sorting and matching games where you talk about the looks on faces and sort happy and sad faces. Introduce new emotions, such as surprise or anger, over time.
- Help her recognize words for feelings by emphasizing them in your speech and putting them at the end of the sentence.
- Take the toddler's feelings seriously and discuss them with her.
- Let her imitate emotions.

SKILLS FOSTERED:

- Body awareness
- Cognitive skills
- Fine motor skills
- Talking
- Understanding

MATERIALS:

Colored paper
Glue
Marker or crayon
Wooden craft sticks
2 bags or boxes
Scissors

Preparation: Cut six big butterflies or circles from the colored paper. Start with one color only; later add another one. Draw a happy or sad face on each shape. Glue them onto wooden craft sticks. Put the happy faces in one bag and the sad faces in the other.

WHAT TO DO:

1. Label feelings and describe expressions on faces:
   - Start with happy faces. Pull one face from the bag at a time, emphasizing the feeling word and describing it: "See, a face! It is **smiling**! Its mouth is going up." Point to it. "It is **happy**. See, I am **happy**, too." Smile. Ask her, "Can you be **happy** and **smile**?" Continue pulling out one face at a time, discussing how its expression shows how it feels. Discuss what makes the faces look happy.
   - Take out sad faces. Again, pull out one face at a time, emphasize the feelings word, and describe it: "See, a new face. This one looks different. It is **not** smiling." Make a sad face yourself. "Its mouth is hanging down." Point to it. "It is **sad**! See, I can look **sad**, too." Show a droopy mouth. "Can you make a **sad** face?" Continue pulling out one face at a time and discussing what makes them all look sad.
   - Contrast a face pair. Hold up a happy and a sad face and point out their differences. Label their feelings, and describe them.
2. Spread out four to six happy and sad faces. Hold up one face, describe it, label its feeling, and ask the child to find a match. If she

matches yours, praise her and compare the faces—they both smile and are happy. Repeat the same activity for a sad face. Continue as long as the child has fun. Give her a choice and ask, "Is this face **happy** or is it **sad**?" This encourages her to name the feeling.

3. Put all of the faces in a bag. Put a happy and a sad face on the wall at a good distance from each other. Ask the child to find all the happy faces in the bag and put them with the happy face on the wall. Do the same for the sad faces. Help the child when needed, and explain why a face goes where: "See this one is **smiling.** Its mouth goes up. It is **happy**. It needs to go to the other happy faces."

4. Mix up all faces on the floor, and ask the child to find happy and sad ones for you. This lets you assess whether she understands the feelings words without any cues.

5. Pick up a face and give the child a choice to say how it feels.

How can I help a child understand emotions?

The ability to be concerned for others goes along with a toddler's increasing self-awareness, perspective-taking skills, and better regulation of her own emotions. A child this age is realizing that her own feelings and desires can be different from those of others. Have lots of visual helpers, such as picture books, where emotions are shown in a clear way. Look at these with the child, and use concrete language to describe how you know what the person is feeling. Discuss emotions so your child can learn to understand and talk about her own feelings.

WHAT TO LOOK FOR:
- ❍ Does she match different emotions to faces?
- ❍ Can she copy emotions, such as smiling when you smile?
- ❍ Does she start to show empathy when you are not feeling well by making a sad face, bringing a bandage, or asking what's wrong?
- ❍ Does she understand words for feelings?
- ❍ Does she talk about feelings—her own or those of others?

Quantity and Number Words: Where Is More?

Toddlers are starting to understand the word *more* and may already say a few plural words. Now is a good time to talk about quantities while playing. Children learn about number concepts and words gradually. Start by showing and talking about small and big quantities (*one* and *many*) and matching small number sets.

You can make your own quantity book by cutting out several pictures of one type of object, such as cars or fruit, from a magazine. Glue one car on one piece of paper, two cars on another paper, three cars on another, and so on. For durability, cover the pages with clear contact paper. Punch holes along one side of the papers, and tie the pages together with ribbon.

GOALS:

○ Contrast quantities using identical or similar-looking objects to help her understand quantity and number words.

○ Contrast small quantities versus big quantities to illustrate *one* and *many*.

○ Talk about number words in concrete ways: Show the child two things while you say the word *two* to help her learn that number words refer to a *specific* quantity of things.

○ Play matching games, asking the child to match quantities of things you show her.

○ Talk about and show quantity differences when playing or reading books.

○ Give her opportunities to practice answering questions such as, "Where is *more*?" and "Where is just *one*?"

SKILLS FOSTERED:

○ Cognitive skills
○ Fine motor skills
○ Tactile awareness
○ Talking
○ Understanding
○ Visual discrimination

MATERIALS:

5 finger puppets of the same kind (such as frogs)

5 finger puppets of a different kind (such as birds)

2 plates

Sets of similar objects, such as stones or buttons

Picture book that teaches quantity

WHAT TO DO:

1. Contrast *one* and *more* to help the child understand the concept of the words. Using five finger puppets of the same kind (all frogs, for example), ask the child to help you: "Can you help me put on the frogs? Can you put **one** frog on this hand? Let's put **all the other** frogs on the other hand." Count the frogs on each hand: "See, here I have **one** frog, and here I have one, two, three, four frogs." Point to each frog as you count. "This hand has **more** frogs." Then summarize **one** frog (wiggle it) and **more** frogs (wiggle them). Ask which hand has more. Wait for the child's response, and then wiggle the hand with more puppets and say, "There are **more** frogs here." Count them and contrast them to the hand with just one. Ask her to show you the hand with one frog. Wiggle the hand with only one frog. Then shuffle the finger puppets back and forth between your hands. Have the child put the puppets on her fingers, too.

2. Spread four finger puppets of the same kind on the floor. Put one on your finger. Say, "I have **one** birdie on my finger. Can you also put **one** birdie on your finger? Now, I have **one** birdie, and you have **one** birdie." Play with the puppets, and then take them off and start over. Do the same for two, and make role plays where the puppets talk or kiss.

    Next, spread two different kinds of finger puppets, such as birds and frogs, on the floor. Say what you are doing: "Let's put on **two** frogs. Can you put on **two** frogs?" She has to match not just the quantity but also the kind of object.

3. Show the child what objects (puppets, stones, buttons) you are going to hide, and have her close her eyes. Put one object in one hand, and four of the same kind in the other. Open your hands and have her feel—still with her eyes closed—the things in each hand as you ask questions about *more* versus *one*: "Where can you feel **more** things? Show me the hand that has **more** things." Or ask, "Where is the hand with only **one** frog?" She will learn that *one* feels very different from *more*.

4. Look at a quantity book that contrasts one thing and many things (one pig versus four pigs, for example). Talk about the differences using plural and number words: "There's **one** pig. There are **many** pigs—one, two, three, four pigs." Point to each of them as you say the number.

Safety Note: Remove all the finger puppets when you are done playing together. Never leave a child unsupervised with finger puppets or other small objects that may pose a choking hazard.

> ### When should I start counting with a child?
>
> You can count any time now. A child may copy and count with you. Two-year-olds often count up to three or more, typically connected to a routine action such as going down stairs, counting blocks as they are put away, and so on. However, they do not understand that a specific number relates to a specific set of things, such as the number three goes with three things. They are good at copying, memorizing, and reciting sequences, but that is different from fully understanding number concepts.

> **WHAT TO LOOK FOR:**
> - Does she say quantity words such as *more* and *one*?
> - Does she understand clear differences in quantity, such as four things is more than one thing?
> - Does she say number words or has she started to count (even if she doesn't get the numbers right)?
> - Does she have ways to talk about more than one object?

The Third Year: The Year of True Conversations

The third year is magical because a toddler becomes a true conversationalist. Whether he is claiming his ownership rights, talking about last year's Halloween, or telling himself that he is not scared, his communication skills progress in leaps and bounds. From articulation to words to grammatical structures to pretend play, he uses his language differently than he has before. He also will challenge you with temper tantrums and his burning desire to understand the world around him. His language is now so good that it gives you insight into his logic and the way he sees the world. Despite all of this progress, he still needs you to notice and expand on his words and ideas. You continue to shape his language skills. It is time to get even more specific and descriptive, to engage with his imaginative play, to ask lots of open-ended questions, to tell him stories and read with him. Such language-rich conversations will push his language and thinking forward and will strengthen your bond.

Since children's individual language skills vary so much at this age, this section deliberately discusses the year from twenty-four to thirty-six months as a whole.

○ **A child learns to direct conversations and play.** From two to three years old, he grows into a very sophisticated talker and thinker. He is much easier to understand, articulating words more clearly and learning new words at lightning speed. His words are more specific and diverse than before. He knows words for color and size, quantity and number, feelings, and more. He loves wordplay, starts to analyze words, enjoys rhymes and silly talk, and builds an awareness of sounds.

○ **His speech is more complex.** He says longer sentences and adds grammatical words (pronouns, articles, and so on) and endings, such as the plural *s*, the past *ed*, the possessive *'s*, and so on. As he discovers regularities in his language, he will say things such as, "Mommy buyed a bicycle," or "This is myse." Do not worry about such wrong forms! They indicate that the child is working on understanding the patterns in his language, figuring out how to use grammatical structures and new words. You will notice that his language makes a lot more sense.

○ **Empathy and make-believe play reach new heights at this age.** A toddler wants to help if somebody is not having a good day; he expresses suggestions, such as, "I get a Band-Aid for you." He invites imaginary friends to play or pretends to be a caring mommy or doctor who helps sick children and pets.

○ **By the end of the third year, a toddler can keep the conversation rolling.** He does most of the talking and knows how to use language to get things done. His communication skills are flourishing, and he uses language to make new friends, regulate his emotions, structure his play, and let you see into his thinking. He has developed into a prolific and entertaining communicator in just three short years.

Twenty-Four Months and Up—Developing Grammar and Language Play

7

Science Peek

Grover Whitehurst and colleagues looked at two groups of parents who already regularly read books with their toddlers aged twenty-one to thirty-five months. One group of parents was asked to continue reading as usual. The other group received a crash course in dialogic reading. Dialogic reading *involves having a dialogue, or conversation, about the book with the child. In dialogic reading you go beyond reading the printed words and include the child as much as possible by asking lots of open-ended questions and expanding on the child's ideas and language.*

At the start of the study, the toddlers had comparable language skills. After one month, the dialogic-reading group zoomed ahead of their peers in the other group in several language measures. Nine months later, when the last tests were given, toddlers of dialogic readers were still ahead.

Dialogic reading does more than just boost language; it helps you really tune in to the child and have fun together, and this strengthens bonding as well. So, interact and engage with the child in lots of lively conversations about books.

Between the ages of two and three, children's language, imagination, and logic bloom. They generally understand yes-or-no questions, as well as *what, where*, and *who* questions. *Why* questions are on the rise, and they may sometimes test your patience. Rest assured that the child is not testing your knowledge; he really wants to get to the bottom of things. Give explanations to foster his knowledge and curiosity. Encourage questions; they give you great insights into his thoughts. For example, I asked a young boy named Alex, "What does the elephant need when he goes backpacking?" Alex answered, "A sleeping bag. No—two sleeping bags—he is big. And a big toothbrush." At this age, children also come up with new words they make up on the spot that are, actually, quite logical. They say things such as, "I am a sipper," when drinking from a sippy cup, or "I am sanding," when playing with sand. The child has begun to recognize patterns in your words and is now overusing them to create new words.

Real-Life Story

When three-year-old Mark visited, he said, "Look, I got something for you." He held out a bunch of white flowers and gave the Latin name for them. "They are flowers—they grow outside. Can you get a vase? They need water or they'll die. Do you want to smell them?"

I was stunned. Before heading off to the playroom, Mark had given me a botanical lesson about flowers and had told me how to take proper care of them. Later, I asked what the word *cowboy* is made up of. He paused, smiled, and said, "Boy." After some help, he got it right—*cow* and *boy*. He asked, "Is there a sheepboy?" We then made up lots of silly combination words, causing him to giggle at our wordplay.

Nearly three-year-old Karina was chatting with a researcher about the use of everyday objects. The researcher asked what socks are used for. Karina thought and answered, "You put them on your feet. You use socks when you have a booboo." She launched into a description of the healing power of ice-socks for her daddy after his soccer games: "Put ice cubes in the socks, close them up, and put them on your booboo!" She demonstrated how to hold the cold socks on a booboo and advised the researcher to stop before the ice melts.

The toddler now often does the lion's share of talking. He is easier to understand since much of what he says is intelligible. His questions, sentences, and play are much more complex than ever before, and grammar learning is in full swing. Old words are filled with new meaning, and he learns new words quickly. How he uses language is so exciting during this age. From organizing his play sessions to regulating his feelings to playing with words to retelling stories to asking loads of questions—changes are everywhere.

Individual Differences

Toddlers vary in their clarity of speech; the sheer number of words in their vocabularies; the complexity and diversity of the structures and sentences they use; and their ability to hold and initiate conversations, bring in new ideas, and engage in pretend play. Statistics tell us that about 75 percent of children who start slowly catch up in the third and fourth years, eventually falling within the range of typical development. Typical development, however, is still full of enormous individual differences, and making up lost ground from early on is challenging. The best you can do for any child is to keep having great conversations with him and expanding his ideas, words, and sentences.

Vocabulary Becomes More Diverse, Specific, and Abstract

A toddler picks up new words on his own and at lightning speed, often adding several new words a day. What's equally impressive is that the words stick in his memory right away! During this age, toddlers learn new words by using many of their familiar words as anchors. Judith Goodman and colleagues showed some two-year-olds an unknown animal and three other unknown, nonanimal things, and then told them, "Mommy feeds the ferret." The children quickly and correctly inferred that the ferret had to be the animal, because they know that you can feed animals but not things. In another study, children were told to look at the bunny on the *deebo* while seeing two pictures: one of a bunny sitting on a Greek column (called *deebo*), the other of a teddy bear on an arch. Two-year-olds quickly learned what a *deebo* was. When the children saw only the arch and column next to each other and were asked, "Where's the deebo?" the children correctly identified the right structure. Some parents reported that their child kept asking for the deebo at home, a clear testament to their strong word-learning and retention skills in the third year. Even though toddlers learn new words quickly, they still need to hear those words in different contexts to deepen their understanding.

A toddler is learning more than object names and action words—he is learning all kinds of words for properties of objects. He may tell you the taste of things, "Bananas are yummy. I do not like bwocli (broccoli). It tastes yucky." His words are very specific, such that he has names for all kinds of vehicles from big rigs and excavators to ambulances, and he expects specifics from you. To develop his vocabulary, weave word opposites into book reading, just as Alex's mom does in the following examples:

Alex: *This is messy. No, this is messy and this is…*

Mom: *Tidy.*

Alex: *Tidy. This is messy and tidy.*

Mom: *Which jar is full?*

Alex: *This one, and this is empty.*

Mom: *Why is it empty?*

Alex: *Because is because it is not empty.* (Note: Although Alex does not yet understand the meaning of the word *because*, he clearly knows the pattern of the conversation—reply to a why question with *because*.)

MOM: *Because he ate all the cookies.*

Mom: *Is the motorcycle going over the bridge or under the bridge?*

Alex: *Over bidge.*

Toddlers are learning abstract words, such as *think, know,* and *maybe,* even though they may not use them correctly at first. For example, a toddler may add little words such as *maybe* when answering a question: "What do you want to do today?" "I go to the playground, maybe." Or, "I play with my trains, maybe." The toddler may emphasize and exaggerate these words because he has noticed that they get the adult's attention. At this stage, it does not matter whether or not the child uses abstract words correctly; what does matter is that you introduce more abstract words in your conversations. This is also a great time to talk in more detail about feelings—sad, happy, frustrated, surprised, and so forth—which are also abstract concepts. Knowing how to talk about feelings will help a child to better regulate his emotions.

Coining New Words

Toddlers are creative when it comes to making up new words. These often funny creations show that the toddler is on the right track. His brain has been sifting through all of the conversations and words he has been hearing, and he has recognized structural regularities. He uses these patterns to construct his own words. For example, Alex scolded his cat, "Quit nerving me, Shasta!" Later, while looking at a picture book with his mom, he said, "Look, he is sanding (digging in the sand)," and "She is blocking (building with blocks)." He described what his sister was doing: "She is putewing (working on the computer)."

Such words are quite ingenious! We have watering, dusting, working, so why not just add *ing* to any noun to make it into a verb? Toddlers also create new names for people out of verbs—for example, "She is a cooker (for someone who cooks)," or "I am a muffin eater"; and so on.

Such regular word creations are called *overgeneralizations*. They make a toddler's grammar simpler and more regular and logical. Overgeneralizations indicate great progress because the child has found patterns in the sea of words. They also clearly show that language learning goes way beyond imitation. How much a child overgeneralizes and when such regularized words show up vary from child to child. Generally, toddlers need a critical mass of certain words before they can discover patterns. That is why building a vocabulary quickly is important.

Toddlers also love to talk about moms and babies; hence, terms such as *mama bear, baby bear, mama lion,* and *baby lion;* using *mama* to talk about big things and *baby* to talk about little things. When coming up with new words, toddlers sometimes are very specific, saying things such as *Mercedes car, 'rarri car* (Ferrari), *taxi car,* or *poodle dog.*

They engage in role play and talk with imaginary friends, asking their invisible guests, "Want some juice—owange juice or apple juice?" You may also notice that the toddler has endearing conversations with his stuffed animals, discussing whether they want baths or snacks.

Playing with Language

Make up silly words with a toddler, such as *aageedeega,* or ask him silly questions and make silly statements such as, "I like to eat pizza with mud sprinkles," or, "I have toast and shoes for breakfast. How about you?" Such language play is not only fun, but it also gets a toddler to really think about language and explore sounds and words. He will soon make up his own silly sounds and sentences. Additionally, toddlers love to listen to rhyming words in songs and stories, because they are becoming more aware of the sounds in words and are learning to experiment with and manipulate them.

Some toddlers may analyze and take words apart, just as Mark did when he asked me about a *sheepboy* as opposed to a cowboy. All their questions clearly show that they are digging deeper into language. In doing so, they come up with very logical new words.

They also crack their first jokes and say things they know are untrue just to see how you will react. Some of your words may get them thinking, just as when I said to Julia as she was leaving, "See you later, alligator!" She looked at me long and hard and then turned to her mom and whispered, "Mom, I am not alligator. I am Julia."

Getting Things Done and Solving Problems with Words

Toddlers now use words to accomplish tasks and solve problems. They initiate conversations. They direct you, saying things such as, "Mommy, put the puzzle in there." They tell you if you do not do things the right way: "No, Daddy, this is wong (wrong)—it does not work this way!" They expand what you say, "This is not a truck—it is a garbage truck." They ask all kinds of questions, such as, "Where does the garbage go?" They show off what they can do: "Look, I am a strong boy. I walk up the hill." They inquire about your feelings and state how they feel, "Mom, are you sad? I am not sad today! I am happy!" They politely invite you to a party and tell you what to bring.

Logic begins to bloom, and they quickly solve problems using language—for example, when Alex's mom said, "I cannot give you ice cubes; my hands are dirty," he replied, "Wash hands and then give ice cubes." When Jon asked where the water goes when it leaves the bathtub, his mom explained that it goes down the drain. Later on, after eating some candy, he remarked that the candy had gone down the drain, too.

Using Words to Regulate Actions and Emotions

A toddler may use words and sentences to instruct himself, "Put hat on this chair!" or "Hold it!" He may use language to remind himself what not to do, such as saying, "Do not spill! Hold tight!" as he carries a glass of water. He also uses his words to regulate his emotions and to soothe himself. When something scary happens, for example, he may say, "I am not scared! I am not scared!" while grabbing a pillow and hiding his face. A toddler's amazing language skills help him through challenges and fears he encounters in everyday life.

Sentences Become Longer, More Complex, and Diverse

Generally, toddlers should be combining at least some words by age two. Over the next year, their sentences will grow—how much depends on where they started at age two. Some toddlers may combine a few words and slowly expand those. Others will combine lots of words and say endlessly long sentences, piling up words: "I played with my trains, and I slept, and we sang songs, and…."

Although some grammatical endings and words may have snuck into a toddler's talk before age two, now they flourish. This gives a child's talk a much more adult-like flair, making it more nuanced and correct. A toddler says things such as, "This is the bunny's hat! It is not my hat." Or, "I am making blueberry muffins." Or, "I've got a red ball. What have you got?" His sentences and questions are diverse, and he can talk about nearly anything he wants. He is particularly interested in asking you *why* questions: "Why is the car green? Why are your hands big? Why is water wet?" He expects answers from you because he really wants to know. So, answer his questions as best as you can. (You can always consult the Internet, if necessary.)

Ask him questions as well. At first, he will not answer *why* questions correctly all the time. He probably knows that you answer them starting with *because,* so the question, "Why is the bunny happy?" may yield the answer, "Because the bunny happy." Soon, he will get the hang of it and start answering correctly. By asking open-ended questions when you read or play with a child, you help him build more complex language, teach him how to ask questions in different ways, and build his vocabulary.

Toddlers grapple with words such as *tomorrow, soon,* and *before,* asking you questions such as, "When is tomorrow? Is tomorrow soon?" A child may not understand time words accurately for a while, but his questions indicate that he is working on them. Although he has talked about past events since his second year, he can now do it with more nuance and detail. Science tells us that reminiscing about the past is a wonderful way to practice language skills and to build solid autobiographical memories. Engage his language and memory skills by asking specific questions about past events, such as, "What were you dressed as last Halloween? Look, see the picture. Who joined you for trick-or-treating?"

Toddlers' Speech Becomes More Intelligible

From two to three years old, toddlers pronounce words and sentences more and more accurately. They no longer drop as many unstressed syllables—for example, they say *banana* instead of *nana,* and *elephant* instead of *phant.* They also add unstressed articles, such as *the* and *a.* Parents should understand about 50 to 75 percent of what their child says at age two, and that should increase to about 90 percent by age three. By age four, most of what a child says should be intelligible to strangers as well.

Words that have complicated consonant clusters, such as /spr/ in *sprinkle* or /br/ in *broccoli,* are still hard to get out right. Mispronunciations remain in difficult words, and a toddler will take more time to master them. Remember, it takes about seven to eight years for all sounds to be mastered in a child's primary language.

Being able to say things clearly is important for everyday conversations, and especially so for the self-esteem of a child. Children who struggle to make themselves understood become frustrated. And at this age, they may face scrutinizing, matter-of-fact questions from older peers, such as when I overheard a five-year-old asking a three-year-old with speech problems, "Why are you talking like a baby?" If you have difficulties understanding most of what a child between the ages of two and three says, seek out a specialist. It may be a motor problem, and the sooner you start working on it, the sooner the child can benefit.

There are also ways you can help a child make himself understood without asking him to repeat words he just cannot say. Listen carefully to a child's speech: Is he leaving off syllables? If so, what kind: Are they unstressed syllables only? Is he leaving off final sounds of words? If so, is he leaving off all final sounds or just a few selected sounds? Is he having problems with vowels and consonants or consonants only? Be ready with the answers to these questions when you visit a specialist; they can help inform her assessment of the child's speech and language development. In the meantime, here are some simple strategies you can use easily and every day to support the child's learning:

○ Slow down your speech, enunciate clearly, and exaggerate your pronunciation.
○ Play with simple sounds and words.
○ Use a mirror to make words visible.
○ Have face-to-face and one-on-one conversations.
○ Avoid background noise.
○ Follow the child's pointing, gaze, and body language to discover what he is interested in, and then put words around his interest.
○ Avoid overcorrecting a child, laughing, or mocking his speech. Interfere when others comment negatively on his speech.
○ Keep modeling: The more he hears and sees words, the more opportunities he has to learn them. Continue talking, modify your speech, and use gestures.

Understanding Story Structure

Toddlers are becoming more interested in stories and are able to follow their structure. Amp up both your reading *and* storytelling sessions as your toddler becomes more interested in stories, because they foster different skills. When reading, chat about the book and its characters, and link it to the child's experiences. When telling a story, make it up and build it with the child. Engage the child in a dialogue about what you read, and have him contribute to the stories. Use books as anchors for specific, focused conversations about all sorts of topics from animals to monsters to potty training, including both fantasy and real worlds. Read books that interest the child; books inspire toddlers. Research shows that books play an especially important role in introducing new, diverse vocabulary and structurally rich constructions, which help children to build more complex vocabularies and language skills. Reading is good for language learning because it gives children experiences they may not have in other situations. When telling a story, use a simple story line that a child can follow, and give predictive cues to engage him in the story.

Children's early reading experiences with caregivers are good predictors of later success in reading. How many times parents read with their children per week predict how many words children understand and say. The bottom-line: Early reading and literacy experiences count. Many parents regularly read with their two-year-olds; it turns out that *how* you read also matters.

When deciding what to read, do not dismiss picture books just yet. Researchers Angela Nyhout and Daniela O'Neill recorded twenty-five mothers as they read two kinds of books to their toddlers: a wordless picture book and a children's book with text. They found that parents used more complex and diverse language when reading a wordless book than when reading a book with text. In the wordless book, mothers digressed more from the story, bringing in personal experiences of the child and asking more open-ended questions. This made the language richer, and we know that diverse, rich language experiences boost language learning. That said, since children this age are beginning to attend to print—and books with text promote learning about print and letters—it is best to mix both types of books to foster children's language and preliteracy skills.

Children between the ages of two and three love stories, whether you read the stories to them or make them up. Stories are valuable language lessons because they are full of words and language patterns, and they help a child understand the meaning of words in a bigger context. A story, even a very simple one, has a structure: a beginning, middle, and end. Around this age, children begin to understand sequences and to grasp the structure of stories. They especially like stories about themselves. Storytelling can be a turn-taking event in which you allow the child to add details and his own perspective to the story.

Storytelling fosters children's listening skills and imaginations by challenging them to create mental images, an important skill they will need for learning to read. Telling stories also teaches children to make inferences, solve problems, and think in sequences. To promote storytelling with a child, have lots of long and attentive conversations, reminisce about past events, and provide a range of different stories. By their third birthday, children know pretty well what it means to tell a story and can do so on their own.

Imaginary Friends and First Role Play

By now, a toddler is a sophisticated pretender. He may assign roles to you, saying things such as, "Mommy, let's say you are my brother. Brothers live in tents." He may tell you that you are the baby and he is the mommy taking care of you. Toddlers may role-play different characters, one time being a sick patient and next being the mommy or a caring doctor who examines sick pets. Around age three, children are often quite dramatic in their performances, changing their voices or speaking like a baby when pretending to be one. Provided that you have shown structured and nuanced pretend play to them, they will break down familiar routines, such as shopping, into minute details—pretending to write shopping lists, unlock the car, drive to the store, shop for food, pay the clerk, load the car, drive home, and put the groceries away.

Language Grows with Pretend Play

As pretend play becomes more accomplished, so does language. Pretend play shows children how to use language to organize their actions and thoughts. It helps them to learn new words, practice grammar, and discuss the future and the past. It also teaches them how to *do* things with language and how to use language in different situations. Pretend play requires children to plan actions and slip into different roles, which helps them learn to understand, talk about, and appreciate different points of view—skills that help them become good communicators.

Children need scaffolding and guidance so language and pretend play can flourish. *Scaffolding* means that you pick up a child's language and ideas and advance them by bringing in new ideas and words, giving the play more structure through language.

Understanding Complex Requests and Questions

A toddler now can carry out more challenging two-step requests, such as, "Get the teddy bear and put him on the bed," or "Take the frog's pants off and give him a bath." He may not always comply, but he does understand you. It is likely that he just has a different idea of what he wants to do. Try to incorporate such requests into pretend play, where it is natural to do things with all kinds of animals and props.

Funny Language, Jokes, and Wordplay

Write down the date and the circumstances in which a child makes up words in creative ways, uses self-talk, overgeneralizes words, or plays a joke on you. This will be a fantastic treasure trove for you and the child later on.

Language Checklist 7: Twenty-Four Months and Up

Does the child	Often	Sometimes	Never
improve in intelligibility and articulation, saying words more accurately, including unstressed syllables?			
combine at least two or more words?			
use grammatical endings on nouns, such as plural *s* and possessive *'s*?			
use grammatical endings on verbs, such as *ing,* third person *s,* and past *ed*?			
imitate words and sentences when asked?			
use a variety of words, including object names, verbs, property words, and grammatical words?			
understand two-step directions?			
imitate a sequence of actions after delay?			
understand *who, what,* and *where* questions?			
use speech rather than pointing alone to answer *what* and *where* questions?			
understand family sets and find odd objects that do not fit?			
use rising intonation to ask questions?			
show more sophisticated pretend play by acting out familiar routines in structured steps; engaging in first role play; and using words, body language, and props appropriately?			
use language for different functions, including initiating conversations, giving directions, requesting things, and asking questions?			
understand two to three color words, some size words (such as *big, little, short*), and words for texture?			
understand size relationships, such as a big doll requires a big bed?			
understand first quantity concepts and cardinal meanings of *one* and *two*?			
say pronouns, such as *I, he,* and *she*?			
show interest in the feelings of others and begin to understand feelings in context, such as why somebody is happy or sad?			
engage in dialogic reading by talking about the characters of the book and understanding the story line?			
understand ownership, such as the difference between *my* shoe and *your* shoe?			
name a variety of pictured objects, actions, and properties?			

Communication Tips

○ Model, prompt, and expand the toddler's talk:

CHILD: He is sick.

ADULT: Yes, he looks sick! Do you think he has a fever?

○ Use specific words: "I am stirring the vegetable soup," rather than, "I am cooking."

○ Elaborate—go beyond the necessary. Say, "There's a little black dog with scruffy fur," rather than simply, "There's a dog."

○ Point out meaning relationships between words: A horse and a dog are both animals. The dog's paws are like your feet. An ostrich is a kind of bird.

○ Model complex pretend play and role plays. Build the language for different scripts, such as going shopping, to the doctor, or to the beach.

○ Use abstract words: "I think the truck is full. What do you think?"

○ Use gender-specific pronouns: "I see Susan. She is wearing a red shirt."

○ Talk about the quantities, colors, sizes, and textures of things. Compare things with each other. Talk about opposites and size relationships. Ask judgment questions: "Is this cup big or little? What do you think?"

○ Talk about feelings in context—what makes someone feel a particular way and how you can help someone feel better. Have the child imitate faces showing different emotions. Ask the child for solutions: "Max is upset. He lost his teddy bear. How can we make him feel better?"

○ Talk about parts of things, such as "Your toes are part of your foot."

○ Use longer sentences and two-step requests: "Get the teddy, and give him a drink."

○ Reminisce about the past, asking specific questions about an event: "Did you play with Maddy today?"

○ Talk about the future, asking questions such as, "Shall we go to the zoo tomorrow?"

○ Ask open-ended questions using *where, what, why,* and *who.*

○ Give choices to foster talking: "Would you like the red cup or the blue cup?"

○ Play word games, and create silly words and rhymes.

○ Sing and make up rhyme songs with silly words.

○ Have conversations about different kinds of books. Choose books with simple story lines and easy-to-follow print. Read daily in the dialogic way.

○ Tell stories. Make up stories that relate to a child's experiences and give predictive cues.

○ Play games in which the child imitates what you say or ask, and then he makes up sentences and words that you copy.

Understanding Size in Context

Children this age likely know some size words. Expand his understanding by working with sets of three, encouraging the child to arrange and compare objects across three dimensions: small, medium, and large. He will recognize and create patterns, practice counting, and learn about mathematical concepts.

GOALS:

○ Help the child begin to understand, judge, and talk about size: *small/little, medium, big/large*.

○ Compare and contrast objects using size words to highlight their differences.

○ Help him understand comparisons and use comparative words.

○ Encourage him to sort objects by size.

○ Encourage understanding of the number concept of *three*.

○ Help him understand the relational meaning of size.

○ Encourage him to build more complex pretend play.

SKILLS FOSTERED:

○ Counting

○ Matching and comparing

○ Memory skills

○ Talking

○ Understanding

○ Visual discrimination

MATERIALS:

2 bags

Sets of familiar things in three
     different sizes: small, medium,
     and big

3 dolls or cars that clearly vary
     in their sizes

Props in three different sizes: spoons, bottles, or cups for the dolls
     or three different drivers for the cars

3 colored squares for beds or parking spots

Doll clothes

Toddler clothes

Adult clothes

Baby doll

WHAT TO DO:

Version 1

1. Fill the bags with sets of identical objects in three different sizes—for example, a bag of small, medium, and large cars and another bag with small, medium, and large bottles. The size differences should be very clear.

2. Give the child one of the bags. Ask him to take out one object, ask what it is, and then ask about the size of the object: Is this bottle **big** or **little**? Let him judge the size. This will give you insight into the child's understanding of these words without any context.

3. Ask him to pull out a second object and compare it to the first one. Prompt by asking, Is this bottle **big** or **little**? Compare it next to the first bottle, and prompt again: Which bottle is **bigger**—this one or this one? Explain the size difference.

4. Have him pull out the last object, prompt him as before, and compare it to the two others. Ask him to line up the bottles by size, starting with the smallest. Help if needed, and compare them all using size words: This bottle is **small**—it is the **smallest.** This is a **medium** bottle. This bottle is **bigger** than the small one. And this bottle is really **big.** It is the **biggest**—it is **bigger** than all the others.

5. Ask questions to probe his understanding: Can you give me the **small** bottle? Can you give me the **big** bottle? Can you give me the **medium** bottle?

6. Continue with another object bag. Line up the objects according to their sizes.

7. Ask the child to sort the objects into three piles: small, medium, and big objects. Ask for quantities: "How many small things do you have?" Point to each of them as you count them.

Version 2

Preparation: Cut out small, medium, and large rectangles to fit each of the three dolls or cars. The size differences should be clear.

1. Spread out the dolls, spoons, bottles, and beds (colored squares). Instead of dolls, you also can use cars with three different drivers and colored-square parking spots.

2. Tell the child that the three dolls are tired. They need to be fed and then put to bed. The goal is that he finds the right-sized beds, bottles, and spoons for his dolls. Guide his play along with questions and descriptions using size words: "The **little** dolly is hungry. Can you feed her? Now, she wants to go to bed. Can you put her to bed?" See if he spontaneously feeds the little doll with the little bottle and puts her to bed in the little bed. If not, help him by describing the sizes, what matches with what, and why.

> ### How can I support learning size words?
>
> Support him by asking size-specific questions, such as, "Is this cookie big?" His answer will give you insights into what he thinks. Demonstrate how the same-sized cookie is little when in your big hands but big when in the baby doll's tiny hands. Use language to describe the relatonal differences: "The cookie is big in the tiny doll's hands, but it is small in my big hands." Grasping the relational meaning of size requires some mental gymnastics from toddlers, and they make great strides between the ages of two and four.

3. Go through all the dolls until they each have been fed and put to bed. In the end, this is about finding a pattern: Little things go with the little doll; medium things go with the medium doll; and big things go with the big doll.

Version 3

1. Play this game with yourself, the child, and a baby doll as the main characters. Provide clothes in three different sizes as props: T-shirts, pants, mittens, shoes, socks, hats, and so on.

2. Encourage the child to try different pieces of clothing on the doll, himself, and you. He will find that even his small shoe is too big for the doll, and your T-shirt is much too big for both him and the doll.

3. As he explores the clothing, talk about what he is doing: "Look, you put the **tiny** doll hat on my big head! The **big** shoe is too **big** for your **medium** foot. Look at these three shirts—the doll's shirt is the **smallest**."

Color Walk

Toddlers love to move and act things out. Here, you combine color learning, print awareness, and physical skills. For an easy color walk, use two colors only. Add more colors over time as the child's understanding grows.

GOALS:
- ❍ Help her understand and say color words.
- ❍ Help her understand new color words using familiar color words.
- ❍ Build print awareness.
- ❍ Help her understand directions with visual cues and color words.
- ❍ Help her understand directions with color words only.

SKILLS FOSTERED:
- ❍ Cognitive skills
- ❍ Fine motor skills
- ❍ Gross motor skills
- ❍ Talking
- ❍ Understanding
- ❍ Visual skills

MATERIALS:

Cloth in two or three colors the child is familiar with

Cloth in a color the child is unfamiliar with

White paper

Markers matching the cloth colors

Preparation: For each color, cut two or three cloth pieces into 10" x 20" squares and two or three cloth pieces into 4" x 4" squares. Cut out small squares of paper, and write one color word on each square: Write *green* with a green marker, *blue* with a blue marker, and so on.

Color Walk (continued)

WHAT TO DO:

1. Put six big color mats in two or three different colors on the floor. Talk about each mat's color: "That mat is **green.** Can you find another **green** mat? This mat is **yellow**. Where is another mat that is **yellow**?" Go over all the mats.

2. Use the little color mats as visual helpers. Hold up the little yellow color mat, give it to the child, and ask her to walk to the big *yellow* mat. Next, give her the little green mat, and ask the child to walk to the big *green* mat. To peek into her color-word understanding, take away the visual helpers and ask her to go to *green*. Now she only has the color word to go by.

3. To support letter recognition and encourage print awareness, replace the colored mats with color-word cards. Ask the child to match the color cards with the respective mats. For example, give her the color card for green, ask her what the card says or what the color it is, and tell her to take it to the matching mat. Explain: "This card says **green**, so it needs to go to the **green** mat." Help her if needed. Repeat this with all the mats you have.

4. To encourage naming of color words, walk through the color mats, and name each color as you are on it. Say something such as, "You're walking on **yellow**. Now you're walking on **green**." First, do it together with the child, and then let her take over and name the colors.

5. Reverse roles. Have the child tell you which color to walk to. She will have to think ahead about where she wants you to go, give you directions, and check that you landed on the right mat. Model first, if needed, and keep the directions simple. Once the child knows color words well, deliberately make mistakes and land on the wrong colors. She will love to correct you.

VARIATIONS

○ For a more advanced version, put a color clue under each mat: The blue color word card under the green mat, the green color word card under the yellow mat, and so on. Say, "Run around the **green** mat. Now, lift the mat, and pick up the color word. What color does it say? (Let's say it is *blue*.) Ask her to follow this clue to the blue mat. Help if needed, at first—for example, "Does it say **blue**? Now you go to the **blue** mat." Once there, ask her to lift the mat, "read" the new color clue, and find the right mat. She can run endlessly through her color course.

○ When she really understands color and size words, add little color mats to the course and spread big and little mats out on the floor. This makes the game more difficult because the child now has to listen for the size and the color words: "Walk to the **little, green** mat."

○ If the child knows shape names, add different shapes, such as circles, to make the game more challenging: "Walk to the **little, green** circle." She has to listen for the size, color, and shape words to land on the right spot.

○ Introduce an unfamiliar color and mat, and see if she can link the unfamiliar color word with the correct mat: "Walk to the turquoise mat, not the red one."

WHAT TO LOOK FOR:

○ Can she do this game with the little color mats or color-word cards as visual cues?

○ Can she do this game without visual help and identify the mats using the color word only?

○ Does she understand two or more color words?

○ Does she say two or more color words?

When does a child learn new color words easily?

That depends on her experiences with color and how many color words she already understands. Children learn new color words easily when they know a few color words well. They can figure out an unfamiliar color by comparing it to familiar colors. For example, if a child sees two trays in two different colors and is told, "Bring me the chromium one, not the blue one," she will rule out the familiar blue tray as a candidate and will bring the tray in the unfamiliar color. This quick initial learning is called *fast mapping*.

Learning New Words Using Old Words

At this age, a child learns novel words without your direct help, using what he already knows to guide him. These activities let you tap into a child's advanced skill of word learning by giving him familiar action words as clues to identify familiar and unfamiliar things. **Note:** The purpose is not about getting things right; it is about playing, having fun, and talking together while expanding his language. When the child understands the game, try playing with both familiar and unfamiliar objects. Or, instead of objects, you can use pictures of objects.

SKILLS FOSTERED:
- Fine motor skills
- Understanding
- Cognitive skills
- Talking

GOALS:
- Encourage him to use familiar words to identify familiar and unfamiliar objects.
- Encourage him to infer novel object names through familiar action words.
- Practice pretend play with both familiar and unfamiliar objects.
- Help him name familiar actions and objects.
- Help him understand situations using property and action words.

MATERIALS:
Variety of familiar objects, such as a cup, apple, and ball
Variety of unfamiliar objects, such as a plastic vase, a penguin toy, and a baster
2 bags
Large cardboard box (optional)
Hand puppet (optional)

Optional Preparation: Make a puppet theater out of a big cardboard box by simply cutting out a window. If you want it fancier, add curtains.

WHAT TO DO:

1. Fill a bag with familiar objects. Pull out two objects, such as an apple and a truck, and ask the child what they are called. Prompt if needed.

2. When the child names each object, prompt for one by using a familiar action word as a clue. Say, "I am really **hungry.** Which one can I **eat**? Can you tell me?" Encourage him to say the name and to give you the correct object. If you are using a puppet, ask him to give the puppet the correct object.

3. Thank him and pretend to eat the apple (or let the puppet pretend to eat it). Continue with other questions and objects, following the same format. Use action words and objects that the child knows well and that give him clear choices:
   - I am **thirsty.** I need something to **drink.** Which one can I **drink with**? (cup, ball)
   - I am **tired.** I need to **sit down.** Which one can I **sit on**? (chair, cup)
   - I want to **learn** some **words.** I want to **read.** Which one can I **read**? (book, dog)
   - I am **tired.** I want to **lie down.** Which one can I **lie down on**? (banana, pillow)
   - My **feet** are **cold.** What can I **put on** to warm them? (socks, sunglasses)
   - I want to **fly away.** Which one can I **fly in**? (airplane, cup)
   - I want to **write a letter.** Which one can I **write with**? (pencil, truck)

4. When the child understands the game, fill a bag with unfamiliar objects. Pull out two objects. Because the child does not know the names of the new objects, and he must find the right object using the associated familiar action word. For example, hold up a toy penguin and a baster and say, "I want to **feed** the **penguin.** Which one is the **penguin**? This one (wiggle the penguin), or this one (wiggle the baster)? Can you help me **feed** the **penguin**?"

5. Wait for his response, then explain why the penguin is the correct choice. Pretend to feed the penguin together. Thank him for helping you and for feeding the penguin with you.

6. Continue in this manner. Use action words the child knows very well, and make up little role plays that give the child a chance to practice the newly learned word in context: "We can **feed** the penguin. Penguins like to **eat.** What else do you think a penguin likes to do? Do penguins like to **sleep**?" Following are some other examples. Make sure that both of the objects are new to the child.
   - I'd like to **pet** the **llama.** Which one's the **llama**? Can you **pet** the **llama**? (llama, ladle)
   - I'd like to **fly** like an **oriole.** Which one's the **oriole**? Can you make the **oriole fly**? (toy bird, ruler)

> ## Why is vocabulary learning so important?
>
> Understanding gets better the more a child knows about and has practice with words. The size of a child's vocabulary is a strong predictor of how well the child will learn to read in the first grade and how much she will understand what she reads. In vocabulary learning, both the size and the depth of a child's vocabulary are important. With more words, children learn rarer, more interesting words that typically express complex concepts. Depth of vocabulary refers to how much the child knows about a word. Once she knows the basic meaning, she can go deeper—for example, most children know what *cake* means, but how many four- or five-year-olds know what *that's a piece of cake* means? The more the child knows, both in size and depth, the more easily she can build on that knowledge and excel in literacy skills later on.

Learning New Words Using Old Words (continued)

❍ I'd like to **drink** from a **mug.** Which one's the **mug**? Can you **drink** from a **mug**? (mug, whistle)

❍ I want to **tickle** the **panda.** Which one's the **panda**? Can you **tickle** the **panda**? (panda, garlic press)

❍ I'd like to **give** the **flamingo** a **bath**. Which one's the **flamingo**? Can you **give** the **flamingo** a **bath**? (flamingo, spatula)

❍ I'd like to **read** the **magazine.** Which one's the **magazine**? Can you help me **read** the **magazine**? (magazine, whistle)

❍ I'd like to **go for a ride** in the **van**. Which one's the **van**? Can you **go for a ride** in the **van**? (van, pencil sharpener)

❍ I am really **tired**. I'd like to **sit on a stool**. Which one's the **stool**? Can you help me **sit on the stool**? (stool, plastic vase)

WHAT TO LOOK FOR:

❍ Does he understand familiar action words (*eating, sitting, putting on*)?

❍ Can he use a familiar action word to understand a familiar situation, such as seeing a cup and a ball and correctly identifying the one he can drink with?

❍ Can he use a familiar action word to understand an unfamiliar situation, such as seeing a penguin and a vase and knowing which one he can feed?

❍ Does he learn new words quickly?

❍ Does he remember new words?

Understanding Feelings

Toddlers this age are beginning to empathize. They are very concerned when someone is not feeling well or when a baby cries. They want to understand and learn more about feelings—why someone feels a particular way, and how they can help. This is the perfect time to use pretend play to have lots of conversations about different feelings. This helps a child learn how to label and manage emotions.

GOALS:

○ Encourage her to label and describe emotions.

○ Help her understand feelings in context.

○ Use pretend play to act out and discuss feelings and behaviors.

○ Help her learn about *why* questions.

SKILLS FOSTERED:

○ Cognitive skills

○ Pretend play

○ Talking

○ Social-emotional skills

○ Understanding

MATERIALS:

Puppet

Bottle of bubble solution

Toy animals

Toy truck

Sturdy paper

Markers in a variety of
  colors

Craft sticks

Tape

Colored ribbon (optional)

Understanding Feelings (continued)

WHAT TO DO:

Version 1

1. Using a puppet, act out a scenario to help the child recognize and label the emotions that the puppet might be feeling.

2. Hold up the puppet and a bottle of bubble solution. Say, "See, Max **got a present!** He got some **bubbles.** Can you blow some bubbles for Max? He likes to catch them. How does Max **feel**?"

3. If the child does not say *happy,* then prompt her by giving two choices: "Do you think Max feels **happy** or **sad**?

4. When the child is able to label the emotion Max is feeling, ask, "Why does he feel **happy**?" Let her answer, and then explain, "Max is happy because he got some bubbles."

5. Ask, "What makes you feel **happy**?" Listen to her response and have a conversation about what makes the child feel happy. Share what makes you feel happy.

6. As long as the child is interested, continue the game with other emotions. Offer solutions on how you can make someone feel better, and share your own feelings, too.

   ○ Sad: "Look at Max! He is **crying**! He **lost** his favorite teddy bear. How does Max **feel**?" Prompt with a two-choice question, then ask: Why is he **sad**? How can you help Max to **feel better**?" Listen to her response, then discuss ways to help Max feel better. Ask, "Have you been **sad**? What makes you **sad**?" Have a conversation about sad feelings.

   ○ Angry: "Uh-oh! Max is **really mad** with his best friend, Johnny. Johnny grabbed Max's favorite truck. Max **screams.** How does Max **feel**?"

   ○ Upset or Sad: "Oh, no! Look at Max. He **fell**! He **hurt** himself! Look, his hand is all **scratched**! He's **crying**! How does Max **feel**?"

   ○ Frustrated: "Max is playing with his puzzle. He is having a **hard time** getting the piece into the hole. He **throws** the puzzle pieces **away.** How does Max **feel**?"

   ○ Scared/Afraid: "Max is going to bed, and it is all dark. He does not like it when it is dark. He hears a loud noise. How does Max **feel**?"

Version 2

Preparation: Cut out circles for faces, and make a happy face and a sad face. If desired, add ribbon for hair. Add other faces later, such as a surprised face and an angry face. Tape each circle to a craft stick.

1. Using a happy face and a sad face, label and discuss the different feelings. Hold up the two faces and say, "Hi there! How are you today? Are you feeling **happy** (Wiggle the happy face.) or **sad**?" (Wiggle the sad face.)

2. Wait for a response, and ask about the child's feelings. For example, if she says she is happy, ask, "What makes you so **happy** today?" Discuss her happy feelings and talk about how you can tell that she is happy (smiles, humming, squealing, jumping up and down, or anything else she does that indicates happiness).

3. Hold up the faces again, and model both emotions. Include the child, helping her act out the feelings with you. Engage yourself fully, changing your voice and face to reflect your emotions clearly.

4. As the child learns to understand emotions, use other faces such as angry or frightened, to discuss. Talk about and model how to work through a negative emotion. It is often easier to discuss negative emotions indirectly through a puppet or prop.

5. Engage in role playing. Each of you choose an emotion to act out and discuss.

WHAT TO LOOK FOR:
❍ Does she show empathy toward others?
❍ Does she understand feelings in everyday situations, play, and books?
❍ Can she express why someone feels a particular way?
❍ Does she have words to express her own feelings?

Being able to understand and talk about their feelings helps toddlers regulate their emotions better and build more positive friendships with peers. Toddlers' early language skills influence how well they handle stressful situations later on. Eighteen-month-olds with stronger and faster-developing expressive language deal with frustrating situations better than their less-advanced peers when they enter preschool. Good language skills allow a child to ask for help and to use language as an outlet to distract themselves from becoming upset.

Are all children equally good at understanding emotions?

No, they are not. As in other areas, practice makes perfect. The more you talk about feelings and give a child words and opportunities to learn about them through play, books, and songs, the more she can understand.

Stories about Numbers and Animals

Toddlers are starting to understand the structure of stories and are ready to learn about number words. Here, you support both of these emerging skills by telling stories about animals.

SKILLS FOSTERED:

- ❍ Cognitive skills
- ❍ Gross motor skills
- ❍ Talking
- ❍ Memory skills
- ❍ Understanding

GOALS:

- ❍ Help him learn number, quantity, and color words.
- ❍ Encourage him to learn about story structure.
- ❍ Act out simple stories.
- ❍ Encourage him to name animals.
- ❍ Help him match sets of things.
- ❍ Help him begin to understand the cardinal meanings of *one* and *two*.

MATERIALS:

4 toy animals

Pillow

Toy truck or a box

Toy frog

Toy dog

Pairs of objects, such as 2 strawberries and 2 carrots

2 paper plates

WHAT TO DO:

Activity 1: Five Animals on a Bench

1. Set out five different, familiar animals on the floor, along with a pillow to use as a bench.

2. Begin the story: "One morning, the little **pig** (or any animal you have) went for a walk. He got tired. He sat down on a bench." Encourage the child to find the correct toy and put it on the pillow bench.

3. Continue the story: "**One** (show one finger) lonely little pig is sitting on the bench, sitting on the bench, waiting for some friends." Ask, "How many animals are sitting on the bench? Just **one**—the pig!" Hold up one finger as you say *one*.

4. Continue the story: "Then a **tiger** (or any other animal you have) comes by and says, 'Good morning, good morning. I want to sit with you! Move over, move over. I am jumping on the bench!'" Have the child find the correct toy and put it on the bench.

   "**How many** animals are sitting on the bench? There are two—one, **two** animals, the pig and the tiger sitting on the bench, sitting on the bench, waiting for some friends." Show two fingers, point to the two animals as you count them, and let the child name the animals.

5. Continue in this way. Each time you add an animal, show the number words with your fingers and point to the animals as you count them, emphasizing the number words: "There are **three—one, two, three** animals sitting on the bench, the pig, the tiger, and the cat.

6. When all the animals are sitting on the bench, go through them and let the child name each one as you point at them. At the end, they all hop on a truck:

The little pig was happy and yelled, "It is fun to have **all** these friends! Let's go for a ride!"

Honk, honk! Vroom, vroom! A truck drove by, and they each hopped on it. Who wants to hop on **first**?

"I do," said the pig, and he hopped on the truck.

Who wants to hop on **next**? (Let the child decide and name who is next. Count the animals as they hop on the truck, and hold up your fingers as you do so.) And off they **all** went! **Five** happy animals driving to the beach!

Activity 2: The Dog and the Frog

1. Foster learning the meanings of number words by having the child match number sets. Model and help at first, showing the number words with your fingers.

2. Set out a dog toy, a frog toy, and two plates.

3. Begin the story: "A **dog** and a **frog** each want a plate. Can you give the dog and the frog a plate?" Let the child put a plate in front of each toy.

4. Continue the story: "Now, the **dog** wants things from you. Listen."

   DOG: *Hi, there. I want **one** strawberry. Can you please give me just* **one**? (Hold up one finger, and help the child put one strawberry on the **dog's** plate.)

   FROG: *I want **just what the dog has**! Can you give me **just what the dog has**?*

   (The goal is for the child to match the quantity without hearing the actual number word. Help if needed.)

   YOU: *Now, the frog also has **one** strawberry, just like the dog! **One** for the* **dog** (point at the dog's plate), *and **one** for the* **frog** (point at the frog's plate).

5. Empty the plates, and start over again with new objects.

   DOG: *I want **two** carrots! Please give me **two** carrots on my plate!* (Help, if needed.)

   FROG: *I want **just what the dog has**! Can you give me **just what the dog has**?* (Help the child if needed.)

6. Continue the story as long as the child is interested. Have the dog ask for one or two items each time. See if the child can recognize the pattern that the frog always wants the same number of things as the dog has.

7. If the child is able to get one or two items right most of the time, add three items.

VARIATION:

Instead of the frog saying, "I want just what the dog has," use the number word. Have the frog say something such as, "The dog has **one** strawberry! Can you give me **one** strawberry?"

Stories about Numbers and Animals (continued)

My child can count to eight, but when I ask him to give me two things, he can't. Why is that?

This discrepancy is normal. *Counting*—reciting and memorizing number words—and *understanding* number words are two very different tasks that develop at different ages. Reciting numbers is a memory task. When the child counts to four without relating the numbers to any set, he is simply rehearsing the numbers from memory. Understanding number words, which is what real counting is all about, is a lot harder. The child must grasp the cardinal meaning of number words: *Two* refers to a set of two things; three to a set of three things, and so on. Understanding that each item in a set is counted once and the idea that the last number stated is the amount of the entire set are concepts that will be learned over the next few years. From ages two to three, children start to understand the cardinal meanings of *one* and *two* and, occasionally, *three*.

WHAT TO LOOK FOR:

❍ Does he spontaneously count and recite numbers? (Leaving out numbers is okay.)

❍ Does he have some understanding of the meanings of number words? For example, when you ask for one item, does he give you just one?

What's in the Bag?

Toddlers are naturally curious and want to solve mysteries. Use a "feely" bag to support learning property words.

GOALS:

❍ Encourage her to guess and name objects without seeing them.

❍ Encourage her to name and describe things using property words.

❍ Help her compare and contrast the characteristics of familiar objects.

❍ Encourage her to ask questions about the properties of objects.

SKILLS FOSTERED:

❍ Cognitive skills

❍ Fine motor skills

❍ Tactile awareness

❍ Talking

❍ Understanding

MATERIALS:

Bag

Familiar objects with different shapes or textures (provide two of some of the objects)

Toddlers learn property words through hands-on explorations and plenty of conversations about objects. Naming a familiar object when talking about its property helps a child to learn the property word. Comparing and contrasting object properties fosters a better understanding of their characteristics.

WHAT TO DO:

1. Put one object inside the bag, and set three other objects outside the bag. One of the objects outside the bag should be identical to the object in the bag.

2. Talk about the objects outside the bag. Have the child name the objects, touch them and discuss their properties: "The brush feels **prickly.** The ball feels **soft** and is **round.**"

3. Ask the child to put her hand in the bag and feel the object inside. Ask her to describe the object.

4. Ask her to guess what the object inside the bag is by feeling it—no peeking! Tell her that the object inside the bag matches one of the objects outside the bag. Prompt her and model questions: "Is it **round**?" "Can you use it for **brushing**?"

5. When she understands how to play the game and is able to guess single objects in the bag, offer two objects in the bag (but this time with no toys outside the bag). Reach into the bag and describe what you feel: "I feel something that is (pause) **round.** What's **round**? Do you know any **round** things?" Ask her to guess.

6. Let the child feel the objects in the bag and describe them using property words. Prompt and model questions, so she can learn to ask for herself: "What do you feel? Is it **small**? Is it **soft**? Can you **squish** it?" Also, ask some silly questions that she cannot answer because she cannot see or taste or smell the object: "Is is **green**? Is it **sweet**?"

7. Ask her what she thinks the object is, and give choices to help: "Is it a **ball** or **shoe**?"

8. Pull out one object at a time, and discuss its characteristics in detail—color, size, texture, what you use it for, and so on.

9. Reverse the roles: Once the child knows the game well, have her put one object in the bag for you to feel, describe, and guess.

WHAT TO LOOK FOR:
- Does she understand some property words?
- Does she say some property words?
- Can she describe properties of an object when asked?
- Can she ask questions about object properties, such as, "Is it soft?" and "Can you eat it?"

Be a Reporter

Language learning is not only about how many words a child says or understands. At this age, it is more about how he uses the words he knows in different situations, called *pragmatic* use of language. Here you tap into this skill by pretending to be a reporter.

GOALS:

❍ Encourage the child to talk about real and imaginary things, himself, and words.

❍ Encourage him to answer both simple and more advanced questions.

❍ Encourage him to answer *what if* questions.

❍ Encourage him to answer questions about self and family.

❍ Encourage him to answer questions about words.

❍ Help him learn how to ask questions.

SKILLS FOSTERED:

❍ Creating words

❍ Imagination

❍ Talking

❍ Memory skills

❍ Understanding

MATERIALS:

2 toy microphones or 2 paper towel rolls with string attached

Variety of familiar objects

Bag

Puppet (optional)

Why use imaginary questions?

Imaginary questions get your child to think creatively, something that can help him solve problems later on. Use imaginary questions to foster his creativity, support language skills, and expand his thinking. Record your interviews—they will be a treasure trove when he is older.

My son just repeats my questions. Why?

Children begin to understand the function of questions—to ask and answer—in their second year. However, repeating words, whole phrases, or questions is normal up to about three years of age. A child may repeat questions simply because he thinks it is fun and a good way to keep the conversation going. Or, he may not know how to answer because he does not understand the question. If a child always repeats questions and hardly ever answers by age three, talk to your pediatrician.

WHAT TO DO:

1. You and the child each hold a microphone. Ask the child a variety of questions about objects, himself, words, and so on. This game is about modeling questions, talking, and having fun, not about getting the answers right. **Note:** Adjust the kinds of questions to the child's language and developmental level. Start simple. Real questions are easier than imaginary ones. Basic labeling questions are easier than questions about the function or relationships of things.

   ○ Place some objects in the bag. Pull out one object and ask simple questions about it, such as, "What's this? Is this a cat?" or "Is this car red?"

   ○ Pull out one object after another and ask about each object's function, how it is related to other things, and so on. "Hmm, socks! What do you use socks for? Are socks for eating?" "Look, a spoon! What do we use spoons for?" "An elephant. How does an elephant drink water?" Prompt, if necessary, and be silly, too.

   ○ Ask *imaginary* and *what if* questions: What if fish lived in trees? Do you think lions like to eat bananas? Wouldn't it be fun if dogs could talk? What would they say? Do you think monkeys wear pajamas? What if apples could drive? Where would they go? Can strawberries take a bath? Do you think cats have birthday parties? Do elephants go backpacking? If they do, what would they take? If the child answers yes or no, prompt to extend the conversation.

2. Ask questions about self and family, including single-answer and open-ended questions: What's your name? How many ears do you have? How many ears does Mommy have? What's Daddy's name? How many legs does the dog have? What do you like to eat? How old are you? What is your favorite animal?

3. Ask questions about words that entice the child to create words. Mime the actions and model how to answer first.

   ○ Who am I? Listen, I am **singing.** I am a great **singer.** The puppet is **singing.** He is a great (wait for the child to fill in the word **singer**). Look, I am **stirring**. I am a great (wait for the child to say **stirrer**). I am **eating** muffins. I am a muffin (wait for him to say **eater**). The puppet is **cooking**. He is a great (**cook**). If the child says *cooker*, that's great. It means that he has figured out how to make a noun from a verb by adding *er*. Prompt if needed.

   ○ What do you call a **truck** filled with **garbage**? (Prompt, and give wrong choices.) A **pizza** truck? No, a **garbage** truck. What do you call a **truck** filled with **lemons**? A **crayon** truck? No, a **lemon** truck. What do you call a **pie** filled with **apples**? A **cherry** pie? No, an **apple** pie.

Be a Reporter (continued)

WHAT TO LOOK FOR:

❍ Can he answer simple questions such as, "What's this?" and "Is this car little or big?"

❍ Does he answer more challenging questions such as, "What do you use socks for?"

❍ Does he answer questions requiring imagination such as, "Do you think elephants wear pajamas?"

❍ Does he answer basic questions about himself such as his name, age, gender, and preferences?

❍ Does he create new words when prompted: "A pie with lemons is a (lemon pie)"?

Can You Say What I Say?

Many toddlers love to imitate, but they do not just imitate verbatim. They add their own personal touches, as Jason did when I asked him to repeat, "Can you come to my birthday party?" He answered, "You come to my birthday party. Bring your stickers, please." Imitations are a great way to get a glimpse into a child's language and thoughts.

Note: Tailor your sentences to the child's language level, so she can have fun and build her language and self-confidence. Start simple. Everything counts as a correct answer. This game is not about getting things right—it is about building language skills while talking and playing. Focus on what she says rather than how she says it, and avoid corrections.

Repetitions provide insights into a child's language and memory skills, articulation, grammar, and understanding. Toddlers filter what they hear through their own system, applying their language rules and thoughts to what they repeat. They may leave out sounds and simplify words; leave out articles, pronouns, or grammar endings; change the order of words; or simplify negations. They may answer rather than repeat a question: "Do you like ice cream?" "Yes, I love chocolate ice cream."

GOALS:
- Encourage her to listen, talk, and build more complex language.
- Encourage her to imitate what is being said.
- Practice articulation and grammar.
- Encourage her to think about language and create silly nonsense words.

SKILLS FOSTERED:
- Creativity
- Listening
- Memory skills
- Talking

MATERIALS:
Colored paper
Stickers
Tape
Scissors
Puppets (optional)

Preparation: Fold the paper into cones, and tape to make two megaphones. Decorate with stickers.

WHAT TO DO:

1. Say something such as, "I want to play a game! I want you to say what I say: **Baa baa baa**! Your turn!" Make a variety of animal sounds, and prompt the child to repeat them. You can have a hand puppet making animal sounds as well.

2. Play around with the way you say the animal sounds. Say some loudly, and whisper others. Say a sound quickly one time and slowly another time. Vary the pitch. Encourage the child to imitate these little variations. Notice what variations he picks up on.

3. Say words and sounds through the megaphones. Talk with the child about how the sounds seem different when they come out of the megaphones.

4. Say a simple sentence, and have a puppet or third person repeat what you just said. For example, tell the puppet, "Max, listen and say what I say. **My bear is soft**." Max repeats, "**My bear is soft**."

5. Prompt the child, "Can you say what Max said?" If not, whisper the sentence to the child again. Stick to short, simple sentences to motivate and make it fun for the child.
   - ○ I eat!
   - ○ I love pizza!
   - ○ I have two eyes.
   - ○ Mommy has a car.

   Add some silly sentences for fun: "Bananas can fly." "Cars eat pasta."

6. Using the same strategy, try longer sentences. First, have the puppet repeat what you say, then encourage the child to repeat. Vary the sentences, using questions, negations, past-tense sentences, or sentences with property words.
   - ○ Do you like ice cream? (The child may respond to the question, rather than repeat it.)
   - ○ I kissed the dog.
   - ○ Mommy bought me a truck.
   - ○ I love big, bouncy bubbles.
   - ○ Do not kick the ball.

7. Now say single words, both real ones and silly made-up ones. Children this age enjoy making up and repeating silly words.
   - ○ Start simple: *ball, dog, shoe*
   - ○ Say silly words: *dub, meep, som, foog*
   - ○ Try harder words: *banana, giraffe, computer, bicycle*
   - ○ Try harder silly words: *nabaka, tonrupa, fleekarnish*

8. When the child understands the game and can repeat many different words and sentences, reverse the roles. Ask the child to come up with words and sentences for you or the puppet to repeat. Reversing the game makes her really think about language. Consider recording the child and letting her listen to herself. This sharpens listening skills.

WHAT TO LOOK FOR:
- ○ Does she articulate simple sounds and words clearly?
- ○ Does she imitate simple sentences more or less correctly?
- ○ Does she imitate longer and more difficult sentences?
- ○ Does she include articles, grammatical endings, and pronouns?
- ○ Does she pick up on changes in loudness or speed?
- ○ Does she keep track of the number of syllables you say?
- ○ Does she imitate nonsense words?
- ○ Does she come up with her own nonsense words?

Why should I ask my child to repeat made-up nonsense words?

Using nonsense words lets you peek into the child's memory skills. To repeat a nonsense word, she cannot pull out a memorized word but must rely on her sound memory to reproduce the nonsense word. Memorizing sounds is crucial in word learning, and children who are better at repeating nonsense words seem to build vocabularies faster.

Mirror, Mirror, What Can You See?

Mirrors are magical for a child, so tap into this fascination by exploring reflections. This activity gets him to name and ask for things in immediate sight and even outside of his line of sight. He will discover that he can see things that are behind him and, depending on how he tilts the mirror, can see objects around him. Mirrors are a great way to get to know each other and to talk about self and others.

SKILLS FOSTERED:

○ Talking
○ Perspective taking
○ Spatial understanding
○ Visual discrimination

MATERIALS:

1 unbreakable mirror that the child can easily hold

Stickers

GOALS:

○ Help the child build more complex language.
○ Help him understand different perspectives.
○ Encourage him to answer and ask questions about objects and properties.
○ Help him learn about locations, spatial and directional words.
○ Help him understand pronouns.
○ Help him understand quantity questions.

Why are mirror games good play activities?

Mirror games sharpen a child's visual attention, allow him to learn about different perspectives, and foster thinking. A mirror lets him see language as he watches how words are formed as he speaks. Mirror games can be helpful for children with articulation problems. Exaggerate sounds and articulate them clearly, and let him reproduce them. He may become better at forming sounds when he sees his own mouth forming them as he talks.

WHAT TO DO:

1. Hold the mirror and ask questions about your faces. "Can you see **my** nose?" (Point to your nose.) "Can you see **your** nose?" (Point to his nose.) "Can you see **our** noses? Can you put a sticker on **my** nose?" Notice which nose he points at—the mirror or the real one.

2. Entice him to talk about what he sees and to compare body parts using pronouns. "This is **your** nose." Point to his nose. "This is **my** nose." Point to yours. Show him that you can touch your nose and his nose in the mirror. Ask him to touch parts of your faces in the mirror. He will have fun doing so once he discovers how.

3. Ask factual questions such as, "How many noses do **I** have?" and "How many eyes do **you** have?" Say, "We each have **one** nose and **two** eyes."

4. Introduce the concepts of *left* and *right:* "This is my **left** ear. There is your **left** ear." He will need time to grasp these concepts.

5. Ask about unfamiliar parts and give directions: "Can you see **my freckles**? Look **close** to my nose, **under** my eyes. These little spots are called **freckles.** Do you have **freckles**?" Continue with other features: "Can you see **my eyebrows**? See my eyes? **My eyebrows** are the lines **above** my eyes. Where are **your eyebrows**? How many **eyebrows** do you have?" Help as needed.

6. Ask about big and then small things in the background. Move back, so he has the full view of the mirror, and say something such as: "Look, is there anything else in the mirror that you can see?" Does the child realize that he can see things beyond his face, things that are in the background? Ask for a big, obvious thing: "Can you see the door?" Or, let him hold the mirror, and sit behind him. Hold up some fingers and ask, "Can you see my fingers?" How many are there? Can you hold up as many fingers as I am?" Wave your hand. "Do you see my hand waving? Can you wave your hand?" Does he copy your movements in the mirror or turn around to you? Ask for other things, giving directions and coaching him when necessary.

7. Ask for things that can only be seen when tilting the mirror, such as his feet. Help him to tilt the mirror so he can see them. Explore and talk about what he can see when he tilts the mirror in different ways—his feet, your feet, the ceiling, the ceiling lamp, and so on. Then challenge him and ask, "Can you see your nose?" See if he has figured out how to make his nose come back in the mirror. Help, if needed.

8. When he understands the game, encourage him to ask you to find things in the mirror. Model the questions and help him, if needed.

WHAT TO LOOK FOR:

❍ Does he understand directions using pronouns? "Where is your nose?" "Where is my nose?"

❍ Can he shift perspective in the mirror game and make a connection between the reflection and the real thing?

❍ Can he tilt the mirror to see different objects in the room?

❍ Does he engage in mirror sound games?

Pronoun reversal or confusion is common and normal in toddlers. Personal pronouns such as *you* and *I* require a shift in the perspective, depending on who talks. Children learn about pronouns through overhearing conversations, watching and attending to how other people address each other.

Sounds and Letters

Children are very interested in words and sounds at this age. Now is a good time to introduce the alphabet and play sound-letter games. Building sound-letter awareness is crucial in learning to read later on.

SKILLS FOSTERED:

○ Auditory discrimination
○ Cognitive skills
○ Fine motor skills
○ Listening
○ Talking
○ Visual discrimination

MATERIALS:

Colored paper
2 paper plates
10 small plastic balls
    (or colored paper
    squares)
Waterproof marker
2 boxes

GOALS:

○ Help her learn about letters.
○ Help her learn about quantities.
○ Build sound-letter awareness.
○ Help her understand directions.

WHAT TO DO:

Activity 1: Matching Letters

Preparation: Cut out nine letters, such as three *As*, three *Bs*, and three *Cs*, or draw them on paper and cut out small squares for each letter. Use uppercase letters only.

1. Spread out all nine letters on the floor or table, and put out two plates.
2. Put an **A** on your plate, and say something such as, "This is an **A**! I have an **A**. Can you find an **A**? Put the **A** on your plate." Help the child if needed.
3. Point out how the two letters look the same. Trace their outlines. Prompt the child to say the letter: This is an **A**. Can you say **A**?"
4. Move the letters off of your plates, and start again with another letter. This way, the child always only has one letter on the plate and can match it with its sound. Once she is more advanced, you can take out two letters that she can match.

Activity 2: Alphabet Soup

1. When the child knows a few letters, play a game with the letters she knows. For example, pretend to make alphabet soup. Say, "I'd like to have **one A**, and **lots of Cs. Cs** taste so good!" Put the letters on the plate.
2. Have fun testing her understanding of letters and quantity words. Contrast *one* and *many* to see if she distinguishes small and big quantities.
3. When she understands how to play, reverse the game and let her order. Prompt her, to get the conversation going: "Would you like to have **As** or **Cs**? How many **As**?
4. Sneak in a new letter and ask for it. Does she match the new sound with the new symbol?

Activity 3: Letter Boxes and Letter Balls

Preparation: Write the letter *A* on five small, plastic balls and the letter *B* on another five. Write a big *A* on one paper square and a big *B* on another. Set out two boxes, and put one square outside each box.

1. Start simple with two letter balls, *A* and *B*, and matching letter boxes. Spread all the letter balls out on the floor.

2. Name each letter ball with the child, and ask where it should go: "Which ball have you got? An **A** ball. It has an **A** on it. Where does the **A** go? It goes into the box with the **A**."

3. Let the child throw the *A* ball into the *A* box. Say something such as, "**A** goes to **A**!"

4. Model for *B* as well, and have the child place each ball in a basket.

5. To vary the game, increase the distance to the boxes to challenge her motor and thinking skills. She will realize that a longer distance makes it harder to get the ball into the box. Add new letters as the child gets more advanced.

WHAT TO LOOK FOR:

○ Does she match letters when seeing *and* hearing them?

○ Can she identify a letter when you ask for it: "I see an **A**. Can you find an **A**?"

○ Does she know letter-object pairs: "**A** is for ***apple***"?

○ Does she recognize her own name?

○ Does she pay attention to written text, such as pointing out a letter as you drive?

When is my child ready for the alphabet?

There is no definite age limit: Some children love playing these games before age two; others are ready quite a bit later. Try these activities, and if the child has fun, keep playing them. If not, come back a few weeks or months later. Remember that learning the alphabet is more than reciting the letters. Knowing a letter is a lot harder and involves an awareness of the shape, sound, and name of the letter. If you point at a letter and ask what sound it makes, and she gets it right, this is a good indication she has letter-sound awareness.

Learning the alphabet is about building sound-sight awareness: a particular letter stands for a sound, and sounds have certain sequences in words. Letters are abstract, and children learn best when they can match the sound of the letter with its written symbol. Science suggests that a child's letter knowledge, especially her ability to identify the alphabet letters by name, strongly predicts how well the child will learn to read and spell later on.

Perfecting Relationships

Toddlers can categorize things into sets, but how much do they really know about objects and how they belong to bigger families? A great way to find out is to sneak wrong members into groups of objects. Can the child spot the intruder and even say why it does not belong there? Can he find the correct family for an unfamiliar object?

SKILLS FOSTERED:

- ○ Cognitive skills
- ○ Understanding
- ○ Tactile awareness
- ○ Talking
- ○ Visual discrimination

GOALS:

- ○ Help him build vocabulary.
- ○ Help him build more complex category knowledge.
- ○ Encourage him to compare objects, finding and naming the odd one out.
- ○ Encourage him to name objects, talking about their function, size, color, and so on.
- ○ Help him understand negation.
- ○ Help him understand *why* questions.

MATERIALS:

2 pillowcases or bags

4–5 familiar toys of one category, such as animals

1 familiar toy of a different category, such as a vehicle

3–4 familiar toys of two different categories, such as animals and vehicles

3–4 unfamiliar toys of the same two categories, such as animals and vehicles

WHAT TO DO:

Activity 1: Which One Does Not Belong?

Preparation: Put four or five toys from one category and one toy from another category in the bag before you start.

1. Give the child the bag, and have him pull out one object at a time and name it.

2. When all the objects are out, line them up and say something such as, "Hmm, something is wrong here. One thing doesn't belong, but which one? Which thing does **not** belong?" Wait for a response, and prompt him if he needs help: "The **tiger** is an **animal.** The **bunny** is an **animal.** Show me **all** the **animals.** How about the **truck**? Yes, that's right—the **truck** does **not belong** here." Ask the child to take away the odd member.

3. Ask, "Why did the truck not belong here?" Wait for a response, and prompt the child if needed: "Because the **truck** is **different.** How is it different? The **tiger,** the **bunny**—they are **all animals.** They eat, drink, and breathe. A **truck** does not eat, drink, or breathe. It is **not** a **living thing.** It is a **vehicle.**"

4. Vary the activity by changing the sets you offer:
   - Size: offer something big among small things
   - Color: offer something yellow among red things
   - Shape: a circle among triangles

5. When the child understands how to play the game, try making the sets harder to distinguish—for example:
   - Within-family sets: a land animal among water animals
   - Verbs: a thing that cannot fly among things that fly; things that you can eat among things you wear

Activity 2: Where Does the Sea Lion Belong?

Preparation: Give the child a bag with all the familiar animals and vehicles inside, and you keep the bag with the unfamiliar animals and vehicles.

1. Have the child pull out one object at a time and name it.

2. Ask him to sort the objects into two categories: animals and vehicles. Prompt him to tell you the family name: "Oh you found a **lion,** a **dog,** and a **cat.** What are they?" Wait for his response, prompt him if needed: "Are they **vehicles**? No, they are all **animals.**"

3. Pull out an unfamiliar object from your bag, such as a sea lion. Name the new animal: "Oh, I found a **sea lion**!"

4. Ask questions about the new animal: "What do you think sea lions can do? Can they drive? Where do they live? Do they eat? What kind of food do you think they eat?" Then ask which family the sea lion belongs to, the animals or the vehicles.

5. Introduce an unfamiliar vehicle next, such as an excavator. Discuss the new object in detail, comparing it to vehicles the child knows: "The excavator has wheels, and so does a car." Ask which family the excavator belongs to, animals or vehicles.

> As their vocabularies grow, children get better at comparing words and assigning things to categories. Even children's small vocabularies already have some structure: The child's brain knows that *horse* is closer in meaning to *dog* than to *car.* The brain does not store words in a random way but organizes words in family clusters such as animals and vehicles. Words that share some common features are put together in one big family.

Perfecting Relationships (continued)

Does it matter how I talk about things?

Yes, it does. When you talk about objects, you can point out how they are related to each other: "This is a sea lion. It is different from a lion. It lives in the ocean just like a whale and a fish do. The lion does not live in the water. It lives on land." If you relate objects, the child can find patterns and relationships among words and can connect them to families. This way, the child can build a larger, more diverse vocabulary. Children's vocabularies mirror their parents'—statistics from the seminal Hart and Risely study show that 86 to 98 percent of the words in a child's vocabulary are those present in the parents' vocabularies.

WHAT TO LOOK FOR:

○ Does he say names for family sets, such as *vehicles* and *animals*?

○ Does he say specific names for category members, such as *sailboat* and *VW Beetle*?

○ Does he spontaneously sort things according to shared characteristics?

○ Does he understand relationships among objects and find the odd member?

○ Can he explain why a member does not belong to a family?

Discovering New Connections

A child knows quite a lot of words now. In the following activity, you will help her discover the relationships among objects in different ways.

GOALS:

❍ Help her learn about thematic relationships.

❍ Help her build more diverse ways to sort things.

❍ Help her learn how to relate things flexibly, by theme or by family.

❍ Help her understand why things belong together.

❍ Encourage her to name and sort objects.

SKILLS FOSTERED:

❍ Cognitive skills

❍ Understanding

❍ Visual discrimination

MATERIALS:

Old magazines

Scissors

Clear contact paper (optional)

Preparation: From magazines, cut out pictures of familiar objects that are related, such as two different dogs and a bone or two different bowls and a spoon. Cut out pictures of objects that do not belong with these groups, such as an apple, a car, and pants. Cover the pictures with contact paper, for durability.

WHAT TO DO:

1. Start with six pictures, such as two pictures of dogs, one picture of a bone, and three pictures of unrelated objects. Spread them out, and ask the child to name each picture.

2. Pick up one picture—for example, the brown dog—and ask the child to find something that goes with that picture. Give her time to choose on her own. Does she pick up the other dog or the bone? If she does not respond, guide her with some questions: "What's that? What does a dog like to chew on? Yeah, he likes a *bone*. So, you can put the **bone** with the **dog** because **dogs love** to chew **bones**. Can you find the **bone**?" Have the child put the dog and the bone together.

3. Say, "I see something else that can go with the dog. What does a **dog say**? **Ruff, ruff.** Who else here says **ruff, ruff**? Yes, the other **dog**. The **two dogs**—a **poodle** and a **Dalmatian**—they **go together.** They look different but they are **both dogs,** and they both chew on bones."

4. Always explain why things go together so she can expand her thinking. The goal is to find sets of three. Following are some suggestions for other matches:

My child puts the dog and the bone together but not the two dogs. She does not quite understand how to sort.

Actually, she does understand. She just sorts differently from the way you do. Children often prefer to sort things thematically. Older children and adults typically put things of the same kind together; they focus more on how two things are alike and share common features rather than how they fit into a theme.

Object	Same Kind	Thematic Fit
ski gloves	working gloves	hand
sneaker	sandal	foot
whale	fish	ocean
cereal bowl	soup bowl	spoon
airplane	helicopter	sky
firetruck	car	fireman
blond hair	brown hair	brush
queen-size bed	toddler bed	pillow
manual toothbrush	electric toothbrush	teeth
small vase	large vase	flower
birthday cake	chocolate cake	present
red umbrella	black umbrella	rain

Note: Adjust the pictures or objects to the child's language and thinking skills. To make it easier, use pictures of familiar objects, and start with two cards per set that have a common theme and match them.

WHAT TO LOOK FOR:

❍ Does she sort objects for their common theme (dog with bone rather than dog with dog)?

❍ Does she sort objects for their family (dog with another dog rather than dog with bone)?

❍ Can she explain why certain things go together?

❍ Does she have specific names for objects in the same family, such as *poodle,* not just *dog*?

Quantity, Plurals, and Numbers

The toddler is likely using many more plural, quantity, and number words than before. This indicates that he is on the right track to clearly distinguish between singulars and plurals. This is a good time to engage him in coversations about quantities.

GOALS:
- ❍ Help him learn about plural, quantity, and number words.
- ❍ Help him learn about regular and irregular plural words.
- ❍ Help him understand singular and plural words.
- ❍ Help him understand small and big quantities.
- ❍ Help him learn the cardinal meaning of number words.

SKILLS FOSTERED:
- ❍ Cognitive skills
- ❍ Mathematical concepts
- ❍ Memory skills
- ❍ Talking
- ❍ Understanding
- ❍ Visual discrimination

MATERIALS:
Bucket or box
10–12 bowling pins or empty water bottles
Old magazines
Scissors
Ball
5–6 pictures of sets of familiar objects requiring regular and irregular plural forms, such as dogs, cats, cars, mice, men, and feet
5–6 pairs of toys requiring regular and irregular plural forms, such as trucks, balls, dinosaurs, mice, and firemen
Glue
2 bags

WHAT TO DO:

Activity 1: Going Bowling

Preparation: Cut out pictures of familiar objects to create sets. Try to get examples of objects that are regular in the plural form, such as balls, cars, and dogs. Cut out examples of objects that are irregular in the plural form, such as mice, men, and feet. Glue one picture on each bowling pin or water bottle. You will have some pins showing balls, some showing cars, some showing men, and so on. Put the pins in the bucket.

1. Have the child pull out one bowling pin after another from the bucket and name the object on it.

2. Ask him to find a matching object, "Do you see another mouse?"

3. When he has found a match, ask, "**How many** are there?" Wait for his response, and prompt him, if necessary. If he says, "Two mouses," say, "Yes, there are **two mice**. One **mouse**, one-two **mice.**" Continue in the same way with the other pins, giving him practice in regular and irregular plurals and with the cardinal meanings of numbers.

4. Ask for different quantities: Can you find **all** the men? Can you find **some** dinosaurs? Can you find **just one** mouse? Use number, quantity, and plural words.

5. After discussing the bowling pins and their quantities in detail, set up the pins. Give him the ball and let him use it to knock down the pins. Count how many and what kind of pins fall—for example: "How many mice did you knock down?" Prompt him, if needed: "Two mice? What else did you knock down?" Describe and count with him.

Children start to understand the difference between singular and plural around the age of two. Early on, they understand that words such as *are* and *some* refer to many things. By using these words in conversations, you can support their understanding.

Why does my child say *firemens*?

It may not seem like progress, but it is. The child has figured out the rule of creating plurals in English: He has learned to add an *s* to the end of a word to indicate more than one. At first, children use plural words correctly because they pull them from their memories. When they discover regularities among plural forms, they overuse their new *s* rule. Overgeneralizations will fade out over time. Avoid correcting a child's use of a wrong plural form. Instead, simply provide the correct form: "Oh, you have four firemen."

Activity 2: One Mouse and Another Mouse. Now, There Are Two Mice!

Preparation: Using pairs of toys, put one from each pair in a bag or box. Give one bag to the child, and use one for yourself.

1. Pull out one object from your bag. Name it and have the child find the match in his bag. Together, name what you have found, guiding and prompting him for the plural word if necessary. Say, for example, "I found a **mouse**. You found **another mouse**. Now, there are **two** of them. There are **two** _____ ." Pause to see if he will name the plural.

2. Keep pulling out objects and matching them up, using number and plural words.

3. When he understands how the game works, you can add a set of objects he is unfamiliar with, such as toy fans. Pull out one fan, and have the child find the match. "Look, I found a **fan**. Can you find a **fan**? Now there are **two** of them. There are **two** (pause) _____." Wait for a response, and say the plural if necessary. If he adds an *s* to the object name, he definitely knows the plural rule.

Activity 3: Which Two Are Missing?

1. Line up two identical pairs of pictures side by side—for example, two fish and two balls.

2. Name each set with the child: "These are **two balls**. These are **two fish**."

3. Ask the child to close his eyes. Hide one pair behind your back, then have him open his eyes. Ask, "Which **two** are missing?" Prompt if he does not respond, and give hints: "They live in the water."

4. If he guesses right, open your hands and say, "Yes, here are the **two fish**!"

5. Play again, as long as the child enjoys the game.

6. When he understands how to play, reverse the game and let him hide a pair of pictures and ask you to guess what is missing.

7. To add a little difficulty, add another pair of pictures, so you have three pairs.

8. Expand the sets so you can practice counting and number words beyond the number two.

○ Does he talk about more than one thing using number, plural, or quantity words?

○ Does he understand the difference between *one* and *more than one*?

○ Does he understand the difference between *all* and *one*?

○ Does he overgeneralize irregular plurals, saying words such as *mouses, feets, mens,* and *sheeps*?

Girls and Boys

From ages two to three, children become very aware of differences among people—gender, skin color, and other physical characteristics. This is a good time to talk about differences in your everyday conversations, to introduce labels such as *boy* and *girl,* and to have lots of conversations involving pronouns. Understanding pronouns helps a child more clearly state whom she is talking about and boosts her social skills with peers and other people.

SKILLS FOSTERED:
- Fine motor skills
- Talking
- Understanding
- Visual discrimination

GOALS:
- Help her learn about gender through gender labels and pronouns.
- Help her understand her own gender.
- Talk about gender differences: "Mommy is a girl, just like you are."
- Encourage her to name clothes and body parts.
- Help her understand *who* questions.

MATERIALS:
1 boy doll
1 girl doll
Doll clothing for each gender
1 paper towel roll
Stickers
Scissors
Tape

WHAT TO DO:

Activity 1: Boy or Girl?

Preparation: For the purposes of learning gender names and gender-specific pronouns, it is helpful to use dolls and clothes that look very different from each other. If you are sensitive to gender stereotyping, you can widen the use of the dolls and clothes as the child understands how to use gender names and pronouns.

1. Play with the dolls and talk about them. Give them their own personalities. The goal is to help the child to learn about girls and boys by contrasting them in different ways and to connect the gender names with pronouns.
   - ❍ Talk about their clothes: Use the gender words boy and girl, and use gender-specific pronouns: "That's Lilly. **She** is a **girl**. What does **she**—the **girl**—wear?" Point at her. Prompt the child, if necessary: "**She** wears (pause) ____." Let the child name the clothes. Introduce the boy "That's Tom. **He** is a **boy**. What does **he**—the **boy**—wear?" Go back and forth, asking questions about the girl and the boy, rephrasing your sentences using gender labels and pronouns. Ask for example, "Whose sweater is blue, the **boy's** or the **girl's**? The **girl** has a blue sweater. **Her** sweater is blue. What color is the **boy's** sweater? What color is **his** sweater? The **boy** has a green sweater."
   - ❍ Talk about their physical appearances and body parts: "Show me the **boy's** hair. Where is **his** hair?" Point to the boy. "Show me the **girl's** hair. Where is **her** hair?" Point to the girl. "Is the **girl's** hair short?" "Does **she** have short hair? Is **her** hair short? No, it is long." "Does the **boy** have long hair? No, **he** does not. The **boy** has short hair. **His** hair is short."
   - ❍ Expand your gender talk: Use pictures of boys and girls with different appearances, and talk about them. Use lots of pronouns to help the child learn how to use them.
2. Ask questions about the dolls, and have the child identify whom you are talking about, the boy or the girl. "Who has blond hair, the **boy** or the **girl**? The **girl**—**she** does." "Who has brown eyes? The **boy**—**he** does." Encourage the child to use the gender labels and pronouns. If the child does not respond, point to the doll directly, and ask, "Does the **girl** have blond hair? Yes, **she** does. **Her** hair is blond!" "How about the **boy's** hair? Does **he** have blond hair, too? No, **he** does not. **His** hair is brown."

Activity 2: I Spy a Girl's Foot. I Spy a Boy's Foot.

Preparation: Make binoculars by cutting a paper towel roll in half and taping the pieces together, side by side.

1. Look through the binoculars at the dolls. Name a body part on one of them, and encourage the child put a sticker on the body part you spy. Use the same phrase each time you name a part, so the child can concentrate on the gender name or pronoun. Say something such as, "I spy the **girl's** hand," or "I spy **his** foot."
2. When the child understands the game, take turns naming body parts. Coach and whisper what the child should say at first.
3. When it is your turn, make a few mistakes and put stickers on wrong body parts. This way you can check to see that the child is attentive.

Girls and Boys (continued)

How do children learn about gender and gender words?

Knowing about gender requires young children to understand themselves, as everyone is either male or female. Before age two, children usually say at least one gender name, and some label themselves already as a boy or a girl. Parents label people with their gender names, explicitly contrasting males and females, more when their child is about two years old than they do when the child is four to six years old. This suggests that caregivers seem to provide gender labels just about the time when children's gender learning gets going. Children often first go by concrete details, by things they can see such as clothes and physical characteristics. This may be a good way to start.

WHAT TO LOOK FOR:

❍ Does she say gender names, such as *boy, girl, man,* and *woman*?

❍ Does she refer to herself with a gender label (does not always need to be correct)?

❍ Does she say gender pronouns, such as *he, she, his,* and *her*?

❍ Does she understand *who* questions?

❍ Does she ask specific questions about gender?

Dialogic Reading

Reading is one of the best ways to foster language learning; build words; and practice questions, structures, and turn taking. Use dialogic reading to spark imagination, thinking, and memory skills.

GOALS:
- Help him build more complex language.
- Encourage him to answer questions.
- Encourage him to ask questions.
- Help him learn new words.
- Help him expand his understanding of familiar words.
- Help him practice grammar.
- Help him practice taking turns.
- Build print awareness.
- Encourage him to initiate reading to others.

SKILLS FOSTERED:
- Letter recognition
- Listening
- Memory skills
- Sound and print awareness
- Talking

MATERIALS:
Variety of books
Toy pets

WHAT TO DO:

1. Select a book that the child enjoys. Let the child help select the daily readings. Read more than one book a day, and read the same stories repeatedly. Choosing the right book depends on the child's interest, age, and developmental stage. Offer a selection of books—story books, books about animals, the alphabet, rhyming books, books about feelings, books about using the potty—any book that you think is appropriate.

2. Dialogic reading relies on many of the same strategies that we have discussed that help build strong language skills:
   - Ask open-ended questions: "What is happening in this picture?" "What is the bunny doing?"
   - Ask *who, what, why* questions rather than yes-or-no questions: "What is the boy doing?" "Who is that little girl?" "Why is he crying?"
   - Pause in midsentence, so the child can fill in words and phrases: "In the morning, the boy drinks (pause) ____."
   - Ask questions that prompt remembering details: "What did the bunny do when he got on the bike?"
   - Connect the child's experiences with the book: "You went to the doctor just like Benjamin did. Remember what the doctor did?"
   - Expand on the child's words and bring in new words: "Yes, that is an elephant. See the elephant has a big nose. It is called a *trunk*."
   - Encourage the child to repeat new words: "Can you say *trunk*?"
   - Prompt the child to name things and describe events: "What's this called?" "What's he doing?"
   - Evaluate what the child says, reinforcing or correcting as necessary: "Yes, you are right. That is an elephant." "Do you think that is a horse? It does look a bit like a horse—it is called a zebra."

Dialogic Reading (continued)

Children's early reading experiences with caregivers are one of the best predictors for their later success in reading in school. Read wordless picture books, bringing in personal experiences of the child and asking open-ended questions. Diverse, rich language boosts language learning. Because children this age are beginning to attend to print, promote learning about letters by offering books with text as well. Mix both types of books to foster children's language and preliteracy skills.

WHAT TO LOOK FOR:

- ○ Does he enjoy reading books with you?
- ○ Does he ask questions about the books as you read or after reading?
- ○ Can he name characters and events in the book?
- ○ Does he spontaneously grab books and look at them?

What if my toddler wants to read the same book over and over again?

Toddlers gravitate toward books they are familiar with because those books feel safe and secure. Read familiar books over and over but ask new questions, introduce new words, expand on familiar words, and so on. Repeatedly reading the same book supports word learning and deepens how much a child knows about a word. Introduce new books when you can. If the child is not interested, start reading the new book to the child's favorite animal: "Bunny told me he wants to read this book! I'm just going the read the book to him now. You can listen, if you like."

Telling and Understanding Stories

Toddlers love listening to stories. Make up stories that give the child lots to guess and talk about. Storytelling lets you gauge what the child knows about the language and the world and how well she understands the story structure.

GOALS:
- ❍ Help her understand stories.
- ❍ Help her build more complex language and thinking.
- ❍ Encourage her to make predictions using word and world knowledge.
- ❍ Help her learn and understand words, sentence structures, and questions.
- ❍ Encourage her to retell the story with prompts.

SKILLS FOSTERED:
- ❍ Cognitive skills
- ❍ Gross motor skills
- ❍ Listening
- ❍ Memory skills
- ❍ Understanding and making predictions
- ❍ Talking

MATERIALS:

Variety of toy animals, such as a zebra, giraffe, elephant, and so on

1 baby doll

1 big doll (to be a parent)

1 blanket or towel

Preparation: Spread out the animals on the floor, and put the blanket next to them. Name the animals with the child, and talk about the sounds they make. Put the dolls next to the blanket.

Telling and Understanding Stories (continued)

Why should I tell stories when I already read books?

Storytelling and reading are different experiences. In reading a book, the text is already there; although, you can change it a bit. In telling a story, you create a tale from scratch, which gives you more flexibility. Stories are full of words and language patterns, and they help a child understand the meaning of words in a bigger context. A story, even a very simple one, has a structure. Storytelling is a turn-taking event, allowing a child to add details and her own perspectives. Toddlers especially love stories about themselves. Include the child and make up a story together. Telling stories fosters concentration and thinking: A child learns to make inferences, solve problems, listen, and use her imagination.

WHAT TO DO:

1. Tell the child that you are going to tell her a story about a girl named Molly and her mom and their visit to the zoo.

2. Explain that she has to find the toy animals that you talk about and put them in the "zoo" (on the blanket). Prompt the child if she cannot come up with guesses herself. Describe the animals clearly in your cues—use sounds they make and talk about what they look like.

3. Hold up the dolls and begin the story:

    One day, Molly's mom said, "Molly, let's go to the zoo. Do you know what a zoo is?"

    Ask the child, "What do you see in the zoo? Give her time to answer.

4. *First stop at the zoo, Mommy said, "Oh, Molly, I can see an animal with black and white stripes."*

    Ask the child, "Who has four legs, looks a bit like a horse, and has black and white stripes? It is the (pause) ____." Encourage her to answer and put the zebra toy on the blanket.

5. *Next stop, Mommy said, "Oh, Molly, I see your favorite animal. It runs fast, is brown and black, has stripes, and roars."*

    Ask the child, "Who is that? It is a (pause) ____." Let her answer. "Can you roar like a tiger?" Encourage the child to roar and to place the tiger toy on the blanket.

6. Continue in this manner until you have talked about all of the animals and she has placed them all on the blanket.

7. *Before they went home, Molly and Mommy went to the shop. Molly saw animal masks and she really wanted the mask with her favorite animal on it.*

    Ask the child, "Which mask did Molly pick? What is Molly's favorite animal?" (tiger)

8. *Then Molly and Mommy went home, and Molly had a souvenir.*

    Ask the child, "Do you know what a *souvenir* is? It is kind of a present from a special place that you take home with you.

9. After telling the story, ask questions about it: What did Molly do yesterday? Where did she go? Did she go alone? Who did Molly see at the zoo? What did Molly hear at the zoo? What did Molly get at the end?

10. Help the child connect with the story: What's your favorite animal?

Tips for Telling Stories

❍ Create stories that relate to a child's experiences, have few characters, and employ a simple plot: going to the zoo, visiting the aquarium, shopping, eating breakfast, having a picnic, going to the doctor's office, and so on.

❍ Create stories out of family pictures, about a child's favorite toy, and so on.

❍ Make stories come alive: change your voice, exaggerate facial expressions, and use body language and sounds.

❍ Integrate the child: Tell stories where you give cues so the child has to listen carefully and find the right objects or do specific actions—ask questions, have her act out movements, have her say a word on cue, and so on.

❍ Make stories about messages—for example, a little monkey always screamed when he was unhappy. No one knew why he was screaming until he used words. Then, he no longer needed to scream. The message: Using words helps people understand you better.

❍ Ask questions afterward to see what the child understood and what she can remember. This gives you the chance to talk about the past, something the child is just learning to do.

WHAT TO LOOK FOR:

❍ Does she follow the story?

❍ Does she guess words based on cues?

❍ Can she talk about the story afterward with you?

Expanding Pretend Play

Pretend play is one of the best ways to introduce more complex language, to foster thinking and imagination, and to encourage social role play. A toddler is now beyond the simple, repetitive pretend play of feeding dolls or filling shopping carts. Break familiar routines into smaller steps, using language as a guide. Specific language can make the play more nuanced, introducing new words and ideas and offering solutions to problems.

SKILLS FOSTERED:

○ Imagination
○ Perspective taking
○ Problem-solving skills
○ Social-emotional skills
○ Talking
○ Understanding

MATERIALS:

Toy shopping cart or box
Play money
Shopping list
Crayons
Bag
Keys
Cash register

GOALS:

○ Help him build more complex language.
○ Encourage him to expand pretend play.
○ Help him use language to learn how to do things.
○ Encourage him to use language in social role play.

WHAT TO DO:

1. Bring detail and structure to familiar routines—for example, expand a pretend shopping trip. Throughout your pretend play, use language to guide the child through all these little steps and boost his language and knowledge. Be specific and ask questions that guide the play along: "I need to go shopping. Do you want to come with me?" "What's left in your fridge?" "How many oranges do you need?" "Do you want soy milk or cow milk?"

2. Write shopping lists together. You write yours, and he can scribble his. He will learn that print means something and will exercise his fine motor skills.

3. Gather your grocery bag and the car keys. Pretend to unlock a car, get in, and drive to the store. Once you are at the store, lock the car and read out the shopping list.

4. Get a cart, fill it with groceries, and pay for them.

5. When you are finished shopping, drive back home and put the groceries on shelves.

WHAT TO LOOK FOR:

○ Does he start pretend play spontaneously, without you modeling it?
○ Does he come up with his own ideas and language in pretend play?
○ Does he use language to assign roles and organize behavior: "Mommy, you are my brother. Brothers sleep in tents."

Tips for Expanding Pretend Play

○ Act out stories that pique a child's interest, relate to his experiences, or build on books you have read. It is easier to expand the script when a child already has some concept and language of what you say and do.

○ Do and describe activities in detail, including smaller steps:

CHILD: I am making cookies.

YOU: Looks like your dough is a bit dry. Does it need more water?

YOU: Now we need to bake the cookies. Can you heat the oven?

CHILD: I put the cookies in.

YOU: Mmmm, they smell delicious.

CHILD: Timer rang.

YOU: We should check if the cookies are done.

○ Ask questions, model, and help the story evolve: Who are you baking the cookies for? What is she celebrating? How many people are coming to the party? What can I bring?

○ Act your role, coach the child, and prompt. For example, coach a child on what a doctor says and does and what a patient says and does.

○ Bring in silly twists. When you go shopping, buy dinosaur food and see how the toddler reacts. Or ask, "Would you like some mud sprinkles on your pasta?" The play does not need to be logical all the time.

○ Introduce new words and situations. For example, when you are pretend driving, say that you have to stop to pay a toll at a toll booth.

○ Bring in the child's language and ideas, and expand them.

○ Be clear in what the roles are, and reverse roles sometimes. For example, you can pretend that you are the baby and that you want to go to the zoo. The child can be the daddy and take the baby to the zoo.

○ Immerse yourself fully in the play, giving it your all in acting and having fun.

Pretend play lets children use language to organize their actions and thoughts, helps them learn new words, lets them practice their grammar, and offers opportunities to discuss the future and the past. It lets them practice using language in different situations. Pretend play requires children to plan actions and slip into different roles, which helps them learn to understand, talk about, and appreciate different points of view.

Why does a child suddenly develop imaginary friends? Should I talk him out of them?

Toddlers have vivid imaginations. From ages two to three, they often invite imaginary friends to their home. That is a normal part of their increasingly sophisticated pretend play, so just follow along. If he invites his imaginary friend for dinner, jump in and ask what the friend would like to eat. Enjoy being part of the child's imaginary world.

Rhymes

Toddlers love to play with words and are becoming more aware of the structures of sounds in words—a prerequisite for learning to read. The best way to focus their attention on sounds in words is through rhymes.

SKILLS FOSTERED:

- Gross motor skills
- Listening
- Memory skills
- Sound awareness
- Talking

MATERIALS:

Bag

Objects that you use in your rhymes—cat, bat, mat, sock, rock, and so on

GOALS:

- Help her build awareness of sounds.
- Encourage her to listen to mini-stories with rhyming words.
- Encourage her to memorize words and phrases.
- Make rhymes predictable by placing them at the ends of sentences.
- Encourage her to fill in rhyming words.
- Encourage her to make up nonsense words.
- Help her identify objects that rhyme.

What kinds of rhymes can I make up?

Any really, and whatever you make up does not have to make sense. Children this age love silly words and wordplay. The best wordplay is when they can act it out, too.

WHAT TO DO:

Activity 1: Rhyming Stories

Make up a story that uses rhyming words, such as the following:

The Cat and the Bat

Mr. **Jat** had a furry little **cat**. Mr. **Jat** loved to **pat** his furry little **cat**. And the **cat** loved Mr. **Jat**. There they were—the furry little **cat** and Mr. **Jat**. Guess what? The **cat** loved to play ball. But the **cat** didn't have a **bat**. One day, Mr. **Jat** went out and bought his furry little **cat** a big **bat**. Now the furry little **cat** had his own big **bat**. And the **cat** jumped on the **mat** and played with the big **bat**. There they were, having fun—Mr. **Jat** and his furry little **cat** on the **mat** with the big **bat**!

Knock, Knock—Are You There, Blue Sock?

Where is my blue **sock**—under the **rock**? Where did my blue **sock** go? It is not on my foot! Where, oh, where is my blue **sock**? Is it under the **rock**? **Knock, knock,** are you there, blue **sock**? No, said the **rock**! **Tock**—**wock**—there's no blue **sock**! Where, oh, where is my blue **sock**? Is it in the **clock**? **Knock, knock,** are you there blue **sock**? No, said the **clock**. Tick **tock**—there's no blue **sock**! Where, oh where is my blue **sock**? I am here! I am here! I climbed up the **block**! **Tock**—**wock**! There it was—my blue **sock** on my big **block**!

Hungry Jolly Miss Rolly Lolly

Jolly *Miss* **Rolly Lolly** *loves to eat and sing, and so her words sound funny.* **Jolly** *Miss* **Rolly Lolly** *says, "I am hungry! I want to eat a* **mookie***." Oops! She swallows, laughs, and says, "Sorry! A* **cookie,** *not a* **mookie***!"*

Jolly *Miss* **Rolly Lolly** *says, "I am hungry! I want to eat some* **lizza***." Oops! She swallows, laughs, and says. "A* **pizza,** *not a* **lizza***!"*

Jolly *Miss* **Rolly Lolly** *says, "I am hungry! I want to eat* **tasta***." Oops! She swallows, laughs, and says, "Some* **pasta,** *not* **tasta***!"*

Activity 2: Rhyming Bag

1. Put three objects in a bag: two whose names rhyme, such as a hat and a (toy) cat, and one object that does not rhyme with the other words, such as a banana.

2. Let the child pull out and label one object at a time. Discuss which names nearly sound the same and which name sounds very different. Articulate the rhyming words very clearly and distinctly, exaggerating the sounds. Have her take away the object whose name sounds different. Help and explain why a word does not go with the other words. You can use letters as visual helpers and lay out the words, then compare them.

3. Make up short sentences with the rhyming pair, and encourage the child to pick up the correct object as you say it: "Have you seen a *hat* and a *cat*? Yes, the *hat* and the *cat* went swimming! The banana stayed home."

4. Repeat the same structure with other rhyming words: "Have you seen the *rock* and the *sock*? Yes, the *rock* and the *sock* went swimming. The truck stayed home."

5. Repeat each rhyme often, so the child memorizes the rhyming words and can fill them in when you ask, "Have you seen the *cat* and the (pause)?" Prompt her, if needed. Try saying the wrong word: "Banana? No!"

> Rhyming boosts children's understanding of the sounds and sound structure of language. Rhymes make vocabulary more predictable and easier to remember, which fosters learning. Building sound awareness is crucial for later reading—having a strong sound awareness is one of the best predictors for a child's success in reading skills. Children with well-developed sound awareness by the end of kindergarten are likely to be strong readers in the first grade and beyond.

WHAT TO LOOK FOR:

○ Does she follow the story and fill in the rhyming words, after lots of repetition?

○ Can she find rhyming words with your help?

○ Can she make up rhyming words on her own if you prompt her with examples?

○ Does she play with words spontaneously, make up silly words, and change sounds in familiar words?

Early Warning Signs—When to Talk with a Pediatrician

8

It is very difficult to diagnose potential language and communications problems in infants and toddlers because they are just building communication and language. Certain fluctuations are normal. Sounds and words may not be pronounced correctly, and sounds may be left out or substituted by other sounds. Some sounds may even disappear for a few weeks or months, and then come back again.

Diagnosing potential problems early is also difficult because early language development varies so much among typically developing children. For example, it is normal for an eighteen-month-old to say more than one hundred words. It is also normal for a child that age to say just a few words. That said, there are early warning signs you can look out for. Early detection of problems or difficulties has a lot of advantages. You can seek professional help earlier and help the child to get on the right track sooner. He may lose less ground and have less to make up.

The language checklists in *Raising a Talker* offer a good overview of what most children who are learning their primary language can and should be able to do at the **end** of each age range—at least sometimes. However, children differ. They develop at different rates and at their own speeds. A child may not be doing some of the things in the checklists because his energy is on another developmental area at the moment. But, if a child seems very different from other children, does not steadily progress in his development, or does not do most of the things mentioned in the developmental language checklists, that may be an early warning sign for potential problems, especially if you have spent lots of time talking with him, have picked up on his responses, have engaged in play and language games, sung songs, read books, and used our tips and strategies to get communication going.

Following are some of the most common indicators that may signal problems. Discuss any worries you have with a pediatrician, or seek a

199

speech and language specialist. Language-learning difficulties can arise from a variety of causes, such as deficient auditory processing skills; poor attention, memory, or categorization skills; poor memory for sounds; or poor motor abilities. A specialist can evaluate if a child is at risk for potential language delay and can determine where the problem lies.

Early Warning Signs

By Three Months
- ○ The child is not interested in your face when you speak with him close up.
- ○ He is not interested in your voice or other sounds.

By Six Months
Any of the previous characteristics *and*
- ○ He does not easily smile back at you.
- ○ He does not make eye contact with people.
- ○ He does not vocalize.
- ○ He does not respond to your vocalizations with body movements or sounds.
- ○ He does not react to loud sounds or noises; he does not startle.
- ○ He does not turn to look for you when you speak.
- ○ He is generally not interested in people or in surroundings; he does not show pleasure interacting with familiar people.

By Nine Months
Any of the previous characteristics *and*
- ○ He is not interested when you talk with him.
- ○ He does not respond through smiles and speech sounds when you talk with him.
- ○ His vocalizations steadily decrease rather than increase. (Note: Some fluctuations in the amount of babbling are normal.)
- ○ He is not interested in objects and does not investigate them with his hands, eyes, and mouth.
- ○ He does not show pleasure in seeing familiar people.

By Twelve Months
Any of the previous characteristics *and*
- ○ When you talk with him, he barely responds through speech sounds. He responds mostly through grunts, cries, and so on.
- ○ He does not experiment with his voice in pitch and loudness.
- ○ He does not show a range of different sounds, including some consonants.
- ○ He does not yet combine vowels and consonants as in *da* and *ma.*
- ○ He shows no reaction when hearing his own name.
- ○ He does not use any gestures such as waving or shaking his head for *no.*

- He does not look for objects when they are out of sight.
- He does not manipulate objects.
- He does not differentiate messages such as praise and prohibition, even if you send clear messages in your tone and face.
- He does not engage in familiar games and songs, such as peekaboo or patty cake.

By Eighteen Months

Any of the previous characteristics *and*

- He does not follow you when you look and point at an object you would like him to pay attention to.
- He does not point to objects or body parts himself.
- He does not yet combine vowels and consonants such as *dada* and *mama.*
- He uses more gestures than words when communicating.
- He does not react to names of familiar people.
- He does not yet understand words, phrases, or simple requests such as "Give me the ball," or "Let's go bye-bye."
- He does not investigate and manipulate objects, putting them together, figuring out where things go, and so on.
- He does not try to copy actions he has often seen—for example, drinking from a cup or brushing hair.

If you are concerned at this point, have the child's hearing checked as a first step. Not being able to hear correctly can affect language learning. Generally, a child who is delayed in babbling, and in the use of gestures and social cues, and in comprehending is more likely to develop into a late talker than a child who does not yet talk but understands a lot, uses lots of gestures, follows your gaze, interprets your facial cues, and is engaged.

By Twenty-Four Months

Any of the previous characteristics *and*

- O He does not yet understand a variety of words.
- O He cannot identify familiar objects among other familiar objects when you ask.
- O He does not point out things of interest when reading or seeing something in his surroundings; he does not point to named pictures in a book.
- O He uses mostly grunts, signs, and gestures when he wants something.
- O He does not understand and carry out simple requests such as, "Give me the cup," or "Put the ball in the basket."
- O He does not yet say fifty words or has not yet started to combine words.
- O He does not engage in self-directed pretend play, such as pretending to sleep or eat.
- O He does not engage in some other-directed pretend play, such as feeding toy animals, brushing doll hair, and so on.
- O He does not show an understanding of what familiar objects are used for.
- O His vocabulary stops growing or regresses.

Keep in mind, some toddlers are late bloomers. They learn vocabularies very slowly but do eventually catch up, especially in the third and fourth years. But, some children do not catch up, and the earlier they get professional help, the more they will benefit. It is better to be proactive than reactive.

As a general word of caution, if a child does not yet say fifty words or has not yet started to combine words by twenty-four months, talk with your pediatrician. It is very difficult to predict early on if a child is going to be delayed, but the more you are tuned in to a child's language skills, the better you can determine if there is any reason to worry.

By Thirty-Six Months

Any of the previous characteristics *and*

- O He does not follow two-step directions, such as, "Get the cup and feed the bear."
- O He does not combine more than two words on average.
- O He does not use any grammatical words, such as pronouns and articles, or endings such as *ing* on verbs, plural *s,* and *ed* for the past tense.
- O He uses gestures more than words when he wants to communicate.
- O He does not ask questions with words.
- O He does not engage in other-directed pretend play.
- O He cannot imitate simple words or simple sentences after prompting.
- O He has very unclear speech that is difficult for primary caregivers to understand.
- O He cannot sustain attention for one to two minutes when you read, tell a story, or play a game.
- O He seems to be in a world of his own and does not respond to actions and conversations around him.

Selected References

Baldwin, Dare. 1991. "Infants' Contribution to the Achievement of Joint Reference." *Child Development* 62(5): 875–890.

Baldwin, Dare. 1993. "Infants' Ability to Consult the Speaker for Clues to Word Reference." *Journal of Child Language* 20(2): 395–418.

Baldwin, Dare, and Ellen Markman. 1989. "Establishing Word-Object Relations: A First Step." *Child Development* 60(2): 381–398.

Bates, Elizabeth, Philip Dale, and Donna Thal. 1995. "Individual Differences and Their Implications for Theories of Language Development." In *Handbook of Child Language.* Cambridge, MA: Blackwell.

Bates, Elizabeth, and Judith Goodman. 2001. "On the Inseparability of Grammar and the Lexicon: Evidence from Acquisition." In *Language Development: The Essential Readings.* Malden, MA: Blackwell.

Bergelson, Elika, and Daniel Swingley. 2012. "At 6–9 Months, Human Infants Know the Meanings of Many Common Nouns." *Proceedings of the National Academy of Sciences of the United States of America* 109(9): 3253–3258.

Bloom, Kathleen, Ann Russell, and Karen Wassenberg. 1987. "Turn Taking Affects the Quality of Infant Vocalizations." *Journal of Child Language* 14(2):211–227.

Bloom, Lois. 1997. *Language Development from Two to Three.* Cambridge, UK: Cambridge University Press.

Bloom, Paul. 2000. *How Children Learn the Meanings of Words.* Cambridge, MA: MIT Press.

Bornstein, Marc, Catherine Tamis-LeMonda, Chun-Shin Hahn, and Maurice Haynes. 2008. "Maternal Responsiveness to Young Children at Three Ages: Longitudinal Analyses of a Multidimensional, Modular, and Specific Parenting Construct." *Developmental Psychology* 44(3): 867–874.

Bortfeld, Heather, James Morgan, Roberta Golinkoff, and Karen Rathbun. 2005. "Mommy and Me: Familiar Names Help Launch Babies into Speech-Stream Segmentation." *Psychological Science* 16(4): 289–304.

Brooks, Rechele, and Andrew Meltzoff. 2005. "The Development of Gaze Following in Relation to Language." *Developmental Science* 8(6): 535–543.

Brooks, Rechele, and Andrew Meltzoff. 2008. "Infant Gaze Following and Pointing Predict Accelerated Vocabulary Growth through Two Years of Age: A Longitudinal, Growth Curve Modeling Study." *Journal of Child Language* 35(1): 207–220.

Bryant, Peter, Moray MacLean, Lynette Bradley, and J. Crossland. 1990. "Rhyme and Alliteration, Phoneme Detection, and Learning to Read." *Developmental Psychology* 26(3): 429–438.

Cardillo, G. 2011. *Predicting the Predictors: Individual Differences in Longitudinal Relationships between Infant Phoneme Perception, Toddler Vocabulary, and Preschooler Language and Phonological Awareness.* PhD diss., University of Washington. ProQuest. UMI Dissertation Publishing.

Carey, Susan, and Elsa Bartlett. 1978. "Acquiring a Single New Word." *Papers and Reports on Child Language Development* 15:17–29.

Cartmill, Erica, et al. 2013. "Quality of Early Parent Input Predicts Child Vocabulary 3 Years Later." *Proceedings of the National Academy of Sciences of the United States of America* 110(28): 11278–11283.

Christakis, Dimitri, et al. 2009. "Audible Television and Decreased Adult Words, Infant Vocalizations, and Conversational Turns: A Population-Based Study." *Archives of Pediatric and Adolescent Medicine* 163(6): 554-558.

Clark, Eve. 2009. *First Language Acquisition.* 2nd ed. Cambridge, UK: Cambridge University Press.

Cooper, Robin, and Richard Aslin. 1990. "Preference for Infant-Directed Speech in the First Month after Birth." *Child Development* 61(5): 1584–1595.

Cummings, Alycia, Ayse Pinar Saygin, Elizabeth Bates, and Frederic Dick. 2009. "Infants' Recognition of Meaningful Verbal and Nonverbal Sounds." *Language Learning and Development* 5(3): 172–190.

Dale, Philip, et al. 1998. "Genetic Influence on Language Delay in Two-Year-Old Children." *Nature Neuroscience* 1: 324–328.

DeCasper, Anthony, and William Fifer. 1980. "Of Human Bonding: Newborns Prefer Their Mothers' Voices." *Science* 208(4448): 1174–1176.

DeCasper, Anthony, and Melanie Spence. 1986. "Prenatal Maternal Speech Influences Newborns' Perception of Speech Sounds." *Infant Behavior and Development* 9(2): 133–150.

Ebeling, Karen, and Susan Gelman. 1994. "Children's Use of Context in Interpreting 'Big' and 'Little.'" *Child Development* 65(4): 1178–1192.

Fenson, Larry, et al. 1994. "Variability in Early Communicative Development." *Monographs of the Society for Research in Child Development* 59(5): Serial No. 242.

Fenson, Larry, et al. 2006. *MacArthur-Bates Communicative Development Inventories: User's Guide and Technical Manual.* 2nd ed. Baltimore: Brookes.

Fernald, Anne. 1993. "Approval and Disapproval: Infant Responsiveness to Vocal Affect in Familiar and Unfamiliar Languages." *Child Development* 64(3): 657–674.

Fernald, Anne. 2005. "Young Children's Inferential Use of Verb Information in Learning New Object Words." Speech presented at the Biennial Meeting of the Society for Research in Child Development, Atlanta, GA.

Fernald, Anne, et al. 1998. "Rapid Gains in Speed of Verbal Processing by Infants in the 2nd Year." *Psychological Science* 9(3): 228–231.

Fernald, Anne, Amy Perfors, and Virginia Marchman. 2006. "Picking Up Speed in Understanding: Speech Processing Efficiency and Vocabulary Growth across the 2nd Year." *Developmental Psychology,* 42(1): 98–116.

Fernald, Anne, Renate Zangl, Ana Luz Portillo, and Virginia Marchman. 2008. "Looking while Listening: Using Eye Movements to Monitor Spoken Language Comprehension in Infants and Young Children." In *Developmental Psycholinguistics: On-line Methods in Children's Language Processing.* Amsterdam, Netherlands: John Benjamins.

Fernald, Anne, Virginia Marchman, and Adriana Weisleder. 2013. "SES Differences in Language Processing Skill and Vocabulary Are Evident at 18 Months." *Developmental Science* 16(2): 234–248.

Friedrich, Manuela, and Angela Friederici. 2004. "N400-like Semantic Incongruity Effect in 19-Month-Olds: Processing Known Words in Picture Contexts." *Journal of Cognitive Neuroscience* 16(8):1465–1477.

Gelman, Susan, Marianne Taylor, and Simone Nguyen. 2004. "Mother-Child Conversations about Gender: Understanding the Acquisition of Essentialist Beliefs." *Monographs of the Society for Research in Child Development* 69(1).

Goldstein, Michael, Andrew King, and Meredith West. 2003. "Social Interaction Shapes Babbling: Testing Parallels between Birdsong and Speech." Proceedings of the National Academy of Sciences of the United States of America 100(3): 8030–8035.

Goldstein, Michael, and Jennifer Schwade. 2010. "From Birds to Words: Perception of Structure in Social Interactions Guides Vocal Development and Language Learning." In *The Oxford Handbook of Developmental and Comparative Neuroscience.* New York: Oxford University Press.

Goldstein, Michael, Jennifer Schwade, Jacquelyn Briesch, and Supriya Syal. 2010. "Learning while Babbling: Prelinguistic Object-Directed Vocalizations Indicate a Readiness to Learn." *Infancy* 15(4): 362–391.

Golinkoff, Roberta, and Kathy Hirsh-Pasek. 2000. "Word Learning: Icon, Index, or Symbol?" In *Becoming a Word Learner: A Debate on Lexical Acquisition.* New York: Oxford University Press.

Goodman, Judith, Laraine McDonough, and Natasha Brown. 1998. "The Role of Semantic Context and Memory in the Acquisition of Novel Nouns." *Child Development* 69(5): 1330–1344.

Goodwyn, Susan, Linda Acredolo, and Catherine Brown. 2000. "Impact of Symbolic Gesturing on Early Language Development." *Journal of Nonverbal Behavior* 24(2): 81–103.

Gopnik, Alison, Andrew Meltzoff, and Patricia Kuhl. 1999. *The Scientist in the Crib: What Early Learning Tells Us about the Mind.* New York: William Morrow.

Guellai, Bahia, and Arlette Streri. 2011. "Cues for Early Social Skills: Direct Gaze Modulates Newborns' Recognition of Talking Faces." *PLoS ONE* 6(4): e18610.

Gunderson, Elizabeth, and Susan Levine. 2011. "Some Types of Parent Number Talk Count More than Others: Relations between Parents' Input and Children's Cardinal-Number Knowledge." *Developmental Science* 14(5): 1021–1032.

Hart, Betty, and Todd Risley. 1995. *Meaningful Differences in the Everyday Experience of Young American Children.* Baltimore, MD: Brookes.

Hay, Dale. 2006. "Yours and Mine: Toddlers' Talk about Possessions with Familiar Peers." *British Journal of Developmental Psychology* 24(1): 39–52.

Heibeck, Tracy, and Ellen Markman. 1987. "Word Learning in Children: An Examination of Fast Mapping." *Child Development* 58(4): 1021–1034.

Hirsh-Pasek, Kathy, et al. 1987. "Clauses are Perceptual Units for Young Infants." *Cognition* 26(3): 269–286.

Hurtado, Nereyda, Virginia Marchman, and Anne Fernald. 2008. "Does Input Influence Uptake? Links between Maternal Talk, Processing Speed and Vocabulary Size in Spanish-Learning Children." *Developmental Science* 11(6): F31–F39.

Iverson, Jana, and Susan Goldin-Meadow. 2005. "Gesture Paves the Way for Language Development." *Psychological Science* 16(5): 367–371.

Jusczyk, Peter, and Richard Aslin. 1995. "Infants' Detection of the Sound Patterns of Words in Fluent Speech." *Cognitive Psychology* 29(1): 1–23.

Jusczyk, Peter, and Elizabeth Hohne. 1997. "Infants' Memory for Spoken Words." *Science* 277(5334): 1984–1986.

Karrass, Jan, and Julia Braungart-Rieker. 2005. "Effects of Shared Parent-Infant Book Reading on Early Language Acquisition." *Applied Developmental Psychology* 26(2): 133–148.

Kouider, Sid, Justin Halberda, Justin Wood, and Susan Carey. 2006. "Acquisition of English Number Marking: The Singular-Plural Distinction." *Language Learning and Development* 2(1): 1–25.

Kuhl, Patricia. 2004. "Early Language Acquisition: Cracking the Speech Code." *Nature Reviews Neuroscience* 5: 831–843.

Kuhl, Patricia. 2010. "Brain Mechanisms in Early Language Acquisition." *Neuron* 67(5): 713–727.

Kuhl, Patricia, and Andrew Meltzoff. 1982. "The Bimodal Perception of Speech in Infancy." *Science* 218(4577): 1138–1141.

Kuhl, Patricia, and Andrew Meltzoff. 1996. "Infant Vocalizations in Response to Speech: Vocal Imitation and Developmental Change." *Journal of the Acoustical Society of America* 100(4): 2425–2438.

Kuhl, Patricia, Feng-Ming Tsao, and Huei-Mei Liu. 2003. "Foreign-Language Experience in Infancy: Effects of Short-Term Exposure and Social Interaction on Phonetic Learning." Proceedings of the National Academy of Sciences 100(15): 9096–9101.

Kuhl, Patricia, et al. 2005. "Early Speech Perception and Later Language Development: Implications for the 'Critical Period.'" *Language Learning and Development* 1(3 and 4): 237–264.

Levine, Susan, et al. 2010. "What Counts in the Development of Young Children's Number Knowledge?" *Developmental Psychology* 46(5): 1309–1319.

Lewis, Michael, and Douglas Ramsay. 2004. "Development of Self-Recognition, Personal Pronoun Use, and Pretend Play During the 2nd Year." *Child Development* 75(6): 1821–1831.

Liu, Huei-Mei, Patricia Kuhl, and Feng-Ming Tsao. 2003. "An Association between Mothers' Speech Clarity and Infants' Speech Discrimination Skills." *Developmental Science* 6(3): F1–F10.

Mandel, Denise, Peter Jusczyk, and David Pisoni. 1995. "Infants' Recognition of the Sound Patterns of their Own Names." *Psychological Science* 6(5): 314–317.

Marchman, Virginia, and Anne Fernald. 2008. "Speed of Word Recognition and Vocabulary Knowledge in Infancy Predict Cognitive and Language Outcomes in Later Childhood." *Developmental Science* 11(3): F9–F16.

Markman, Ellen, and Jean Hutchinson. 1984. "Children's Sensitivity to Constraints on Word Meaning: Taxonomic versus Thematic Relations." *Cognitive Psychology* 16(1):1–27.

Meltzoff, Andrew. 1990. "Foundations for Developing a Concept of Self: The Role of Imitation in Relating Self to Other and the Value of Social Mirroring, Social Modeling, and Self-Practice in Infancy." In *The Self in Transition: Infancy to Childhood.* Chicago: University of Chicago Press.

Meltzoff, Andrew. 2007. "'Like Me': A Foundation for Social Cognition." *Developmental Science* 10(1): 126–134.

Meltzoff, Andrew, and Keith Moore. 1983. "Newborn Infants Imitate Adult Facial Gestures." *Child Development* 54(3): 702–709.

Mills, Debra, Sharon Coffey-Corina, and Helen Neville. 1997. "Language Comprehension and Cerebral Specialization from 13 to 20 Months." *Developmental Neuropsychology* 13(3): 397–445.

Mintz, Toben, and Lila Gleitman. 2002. "Adjectives Really Do Modify Nouns: The Incremental and Restricted Nature of Early Adjective Acquisition." *Cognition* 84(3): 267–293.

Nyhout, Angela, and Daniela O'Neill. 2013. "Mothers' Complex Talk when Sharing Books with Their Toddlers: Book Genre Matters." *First Language* 33(2): 115–131.

Petrill, Stephen, et al. 2010. "Genetic and Environmental Influences on the Growth of Early Reading Skills." *Journal of Child Psychology and Psychiatry* 51(6): 660–667.

Ramirez-Esparza, Nairan, Adrian Garcia-Sierra, and Patricia Kuhl. 2014. "Look Who's Talking: Speech Style and Social Context in Language Input to Infants Is Linked to Concurrent and Future Speech Development." *Developmental Science* 17(2).

Ramscar, Michael, Kirsten Thorpe, and Katie Denny. 2007. "Surprise in the Learning of Color Words." Proceedings of the 29th Meeting of the Cognitive Science Society, Nashville, TN.

Ramscar, Michael, et al. 2010. "The Effects of Feature-Label-Order and Their Implications for Symbolic Learning." *Cognitive Science* 34(5): 909–957.

Ratner, Hilary. 1984. "Memory Demands and the Development of Young Children's Memory." *Child Development* 55(6): 2173-2191.

Read, Kirsten. 2014. "Clues Cue the Smooze: Rhyme, Pausing, and Prediction Help Children Learn New Words from Storybooks." *Frontiers in Psychology* 5: 149.

Richert Rebekah, Michael Robb, Jodi Fender, and Ellen Wartella. 2010. "Word Learning from Baby Videos." *Archives of Pediatrics and Adolescent Medicine* 164(5): 432–437.

Roben, Caroline, Pamela Cole, and Laura Marie Armstrong. 2013. "Longitudinal Relations among Language Skills, Anger Expression, and Regulatory Strategies in Early Childhood." *Child Development* 84(3):891–905.

Snow, Catherine. 2010. "Closing the Vocabulary Gap." *Martha Speaks.* http://www.pbs.org/parents/martha/experts/snow.html.

Swingley, Daniel. 2009. "Contributions of Infant Word Learning to Language Development." *Philosophical Transactions of the Royal Society B.* 364: 3617–3632.

Swingley, Daniel, and Richard Aslin. 2000. "Spoken Word Recognition and Lexical Representation in Very Young Children." *Cognition* 76(2): 147–166.

Swingley, Daniel, and Richard Aslin. 2002. "Lexical Neighborhoods and the Word-Form Representations of 14-month-olds." *Psychological Science* 13(5): 480–484.

Tamis-LeMonda, Catherine, Marc Bornstein, and Lisa Baumwell. 2001. "Maternal Responsiveness and Children's Achievement of Language Milestones." *Child Development* 72(3): 748–767.

Tamis-LeMonda, Catherine, and Marc Bornstein. 2002. "Maternal Responsiveness and Early Language Acquisition." *Advances in Child Development and Behavior* 29: 89–127.

Tomasello, Michael, and Jody Todd. 1983. "Joint Attention and Lexical Acquisition Style." *First Language* 4(12): 197–211.

Tomasello, Michael, and Michelle Barton. 1994. "Learning Words in Nonostensive Contexts." *Developmental Psychology* 30(5): 639–650.

Tomasello, Michael, and Elizabeth Bates, eds. 2001. *Language Development: The Essential Readings.* Oxford, UK: Blackwell.

Tsao, Feng-Ming, Huei-Mei Liu, and Patricia Kuhl. 2004. "Speech Perception in Infancy Predicts Language Development in the Second Year of Life: A Longitudinal Study." *Child Development* 75(4): 1067–1084.

Waxman, Sandra, and Dana Markow. 1995. "Words as Invitations to Form Categories: Evidence from 12- to 13-Month-Old Infants." *Cognitive Psychology* 29(3): 257–302.

Whitehurst, Grover, et al. 1988. "Accelerating Language Development through Picture Book Reading." *Developmental Psychology* 24(4): 552–559.

Whitehurst, Grover, and Christopher Lonigan. 1998. "Child Development and Emergent Literacy." *Child Development* 69(3): 848–872.

Zangl, Renate. 1998. *Dynamische Muster in der Sprachlichen Ontogenese: Bilingualismus, Erst- und Fremdsprachenerwerb.* Narr: Tuebingen. (Trans.: *Dynamic Patterns in the Ontogenesis of Language: Bilingualism, First- and Second-Language Acquisition.*)

Zangl, Renate, et al. 2005. "Dynamics of Word Comprehension in Infancy: Developments in Timing, Accuracy, and Resistance to Acoustic Degradation." *Journal of Cognition and Development* 6(2): 179–208.

Zangl, Renate, Deena Skolnick, and Anne Fernald. 2005. "Incidental Word Learning: Two-Year-Olds Can Infer the Referent of a Novel Word 'On the Fly.'" Speech presented at the Biennial Meeting of the Society for Research in Child Development, Atlanta, GA.

Zangl, Renate, and Debra Mills. 2006. "Increased Brain Activity to Infant-Directed Speech in 6- and 13-Month-Old Infants." *Infancy* 11(1): 31–62.

Zangl, Renate, and Anne Fernald. 2007. "Increasing Flexibility in Children's Online Processing of Grammatical and Nonce Determiners in Fluent Speech." *Language Learning and Development* 3(3): 199–232.

Zimmerman, Frederick, Dimitri Christakis, and Andrew Meltzoff. 2007. "Associations between Media Viewing and Language Development in Children under Age 2 years." *The Journal of Pediatrics* 151(4): 364–368.

Index